PRENTICE HALL MATHEMATICS

ALGEBRA 1

Practice
Workbook

PEARSON

Prentice
Hall

Needham, Massachusetts
Upper Saddle River, New Jersey

ISBN: 0-13-063379-8

8 9 10   06 05

Practice Workbook

Contents

Answers appear in the back of each Chapter Support File.

Contents (cont.)

Practice 1-1

Write an algebraic expression for each phrase.

1. 7 increased by x

2. p multiplied by 3

3. 10 decreased by m

4. n less than 7

5. the product of 2 and q

6. 3 more than m

Write a phrase for each algebraic expression.

7. $\frac{8}{a}$

8. $s - 10$

9. $x + 13$

10. $ab + 2$

Define a variable and write an algebraic expression for each phrase.

11. the difference of 8 and a number

12. the sum of 4 and a number

13. the product of 2 and a number

14. 3 increased by a number

15. 10 plus the quotient of a number and 15

16. 12 less than a number

Define a variable and write an algebraic equation to model each situation.

17. What is the total cost of buying several shirts at $24.95 each?

18. The number of gal of water used to water trees is 30 times the number of trees.

19. What is the amount of money in a bank containing only dimes?

20. What is the number of marbles left in a 48-marble bag after some marbles have been given away?

21. The total cost equals the price of the tickets multiplied by eight people.

22. What is the cost of buying several pairs of pants at $32.95 per pair?

Write an equation to model the relationship in each table.

23.

Number of Tickets	Total Cost
2	$7
4	$14
6	$21

24.

Number of Hours	Distance Traveled
1	55 mi
3	165 mi
5	275 mi

25.

Number of Hours	Total Pay
8	$40
12	$60
16	$80

26.

Total Cost	Change from $10
$10.00	$0
$9.00	$1.00
$7.50	$2.50

27.

Number of Days	Length
1	0.45 in.
4	1.80 in.
8	3.60 in.

28.

Miles Traveled	Miles Remaining
0	500
125	375
350	150

Practice 1-2

Exponents and Order of Operations

Simplify each expression.

1. $4 + 6(8)$

2. $\dfrac{4(8 - 2)}{3 + 9}$

3. $4 \times 3^2 + 2$

4. $40 \div 5(2)$

5. $2.7 + 3.6 \times 4.5$

6. $3[4(8 - 2) + 5]$

7. $4 + 3(15 - 2^3)$

8. $17 - [(3 + 2) \times 2]$

9. $6 \times (3 + 2) \div 15$

Evaluate each expression.

10. $\dfrac{a + 2b}{5}$ for $a = 1$ and $b = 2$

11. $\dfrac{5m + n}{5}$ for $m = 6$ and $n = 15$

12. $x + 3y^2$ for $x = 3.4$ and $y = 3$

13. $7a - 4(b + 2)$ for $a = 5$ and $b = 2$

Simplify each expression.

14. $\dfrac{100 - 15}{9 + 8}$

15. $\dfrac{2(3 + 4)}{7}$

16. $\dfrac{3(4 + 12)}{2(7 - 3)}$

17. $14 + 3 \times 4$

18. $8 + 3(4 + 3)$

19. $3 + 4[13 - 2(6 - 3)]$

20. $8(5 + 30 \div 5)$

21. $(3.4)(2.7) + 5$

22. $50 \div 2 + 15 \times 4$

23. $7(9 - 5)$

24. $2(3^2) - 3(2)$

25. $4 + 8 \div 2 + 6 \times 3$

26. $(7 + 8) \div (4 - 1)$

27. $5[2(8 + 5) - 15]$

28. $(6 + 8) \times (8 - 4)$

29. $12\left(\dfrac{6 + 30}{9 - 3}\right)$

30. $14 + 6 \times 2^3 - 8 \div 2^2$

31. $\dfrac{7(14) - 3(6)}{2}$

32. $14 \div [3(8 - 2) - 11]$

33. $3\left(\dfrac{9 + 13}{6}\right)$

34. $\dfrac{4(8 - 3)}{3 + 2}$

35. $5 + 4^2 \times 8 - 2^3 \div 2^2$

36. $4^2 + 5^2(8 - 3)$

37. $5(3^2 + 2) - 2(6^2 - 5^2)$

Evaluate each expression for $a = 2$ and $b = 6$.

38. $2(7a - b)$

39. $(a^3 + b^2) \div a$

40. $3b \div (2a - 1) + b$

41. $\dfrac{5a + 2}{b}$

42. $\dfrac{3(b - 2)}{4(a + 1)}$

43. $9b + a^4 \div 8$

Use the expression $r + 0.12m$ to calculate the cost of renting a car. The basic rate is r. The number of miles driven is m.

44. The basic rate is $15.95. The car is driven 150 mi.

45. The basic rate is $32.50. The car is driven 257 mi.

Evaluate each expression for $s = 3$ and $t = 9$.

46. $8(4s - t)$

47. $(2t - 3s) \div 4$

48. $t^2 - s^4$

49. $s(3t + 6)$

50. $\dfrac{5s^2}{t}$

51. $\dfrac{2t^2}{s^3}$

Practice 1-3

Name the set(s) of numbers to which each number belongs.

1. -0.002 **2.** $12\frac{1}{2}$ **3.** 8 **4.** 5π

5. $\sqrt{7}$ **6.** -22 **7.** -3.4 **8.** $\sqrt{36}$

Decide whether each statement is *true* or *false*. If the statement is false, give a counterexample.

9. Every whole number is an integer.   **10.** Every integer is a whole number.

11. Every rational number is a real number.   **12.** Every multiple of 7 is odd.

Use <, =, or > to compare.

13. $-10.98 \ \blacksquare \ -10.99$ **14.** $-\frac{1}{3} \ \blacksquare \ -0.3$ **15.** $-\frac{11}{5} \ \blacksquare \ -\frac{4}{5}$

16. $-\frac{1}{2} \ \blacksquare \ -\frac{5}{10}$ **17.** $-\frac{3}{8} \ \blacksquare \ -\frac{7}{16}$ **18.** $\frac{3}{4} \ \blacksquare \ \frac{13}{16}$

Write in order from least to greatest.

19. $-\frac{8}{9}, -\frac{7}{8}, -\frac{22}{25}$ **20.** $-3\frac{4}{9}, -3.45, -3\frac{12}{25}$ **21.** $-\frac{1}{4}, -\frac{1}{5}, -\frac{1}{3}$

22. $-1.7, -1\frac{3}{4}, -1\frac{7}{9}$ **23.** $-\frac{3}{4}, -\frac{7}{8}, -\frac{2}{3}$ **24.** $2\frac{3}{4}, 2\frac{5}{8}, 2.7$

Determine which set of numbers is most reasonable for each situation.

25. the number of dolphins in the ocean

26. the height of a basketball player

27. the number of pets you have

28. the circumference of a compact disk

Find each absolute value.

29. $\left|\frac{3}{10}\right|$ **30.** $|-327|$ **31.** $|-3.46|$ **32.** $\left|-\frac{1}{2}\right|$

33. Name the sets(s) of numbers to which each number in the table belongs. Choose among: whole numbers, integers, rational numbers, irrational numbers, and real numbers.

Type of Account	Principal	Rate	Time (years)	Interest
Checking	$154.23	0.0375	$\frac{30}{365}$	$.48
Savings	$8000	0.055	$3\frac{1}{2}$	$1540

Practice 1-4

Adding Real Numbers

Simplify each expression.

1. $6 + (-4)$

2. $-2 + (-13)$

3. $-18 + 4$

4. $15 + (-32)$

5. $-27 + (-14)$

6. $8 + (-3)$

7. $-12.2 + 31.9$

8. $-2.3 + (-13.9)$

9. $19.8 + (-27.4)$

10. $\frac{1}{4} + \left(-\frac{3}{4}\right)$

11. $\frac{2}{3} + \left(-\frac{1}{3}\right)$

12. $-\frac{7}{12} + \frac{1}{6}$

13. $2\frac{2}{3} + (-1)$

14. $-3\frac{3}{4} + 1\frac{1}{2}$

15. $2\frac{1}{3} + \left(-4\frac{2}{3}\right)$

16. $-6.3 + 8.2$

17. $-3.82 + 2.83$

18. $-7.8 + 9$

19. $|-12| + |-21|$

20. $|-13 + 6|$

21. $-14 + |-7|$

Evaluate each expression for $m = 2.5$.

22. $-m + 1.6$

23. $-3.2 + m$

24. $-2.5 + (-m)$

Simplify.

25. $-3 + (-6) + 14$

26. $4 + (-8) + (-14)$

27. $2.7 + (-3.2) + 1.5$

28. $-2.5 + (-1.2) + (-2.3)$

29. $\frac{1}{2} + \left(-\frac{1}{3}\right) + \frac{1}{4}$

30. $-\frac{2}{3} + \left(-\frac{1}{3}\right) + \left(-1\frac{1}{3}\right)$

Simplify.

31. $\begin{bmatrix} 4 & -1 \\ 2 & 5 \end{bmatrix} + \begin{bmatrix} -1 & 2 \\ -2 & -3 \end{bmatrix}$

32. $\begin{bmatrix} -4.7 \\ 2.3 \\ -1.5 \end{bmatrix} + \begin{bmatrix} 5.1 \\ -2.7 \\ 2.6 \end{bmatrix}$

33. The temperature at 5:00 A.M. is $-38°$F. The temperature rises $20°$ by 11:00 A.M. What is the temperature at 11:00 A.M.?

34. A football team has possession of the ball on their own 15-yd line. The next two plays result in a loss of 7 yd and a gain of 3 yd, respectively. On what yard line is the ball after the two plays?

35. Suppose your opening checking account balance is $124.53. After you write a check for $57.49 and make a deposit of $103.49, what is your new balance?

36. During an emergency exercise, a submarine dives 37 ft, rises 16 ft, and then dives 18 ft. What is the net change in the submarine's position after the second dive?

Algebra 1 Chapter 1

Practice 1-5

Subtracting Real Numbers

Simplify.

1. $13 - 6$

2. $19 - 35$

3. $-4 - 8$

4. $-14 - (-6)$

5. $18 - (-25)$

6. $-32 - 17$

7. $-6.8 - 14.6$

8. $-9.3 - (-23.9)$

9. $-8.2 - 0.8$

10. $18.3 - (-8.1)$

11. $-3 - (-15)$

12. $6.4 - 17$

13. $\frac{3}{4} - 1\frac{1}{4}$

14. $-\frac{1}{3} - \frac{2}{3}$

15. $-\frac{1}{4} - \left(-\frac{3}{4}\right)$

16. $|-11| - |-29|$

17. $|-4 - 8|$

18. $|9.8| - |-15.7|$

19. $|-8 - (-32)|$

20. $|3.7 - (-6.8)|$

21. $2.83 - 3.82$

Evaluate each expression for $c = -3$ and $d = -6$.

22. $c - d$

23. $-c - d$

24. $-c - (-d)$

25. $|c + d|$

26. $-c + d$

27. $3c - 2d$

Simplify.

28. $8 - (-4) - (-5)$

29. $6 - 10 - 4$

30. $10 - 14 - 15$

31. $-6 - 3 - (-2)$

32. $-5 + 7 - 9$

33. $-2 - 2 - 4$

Subtract.

34. $\begin{bmatrix} -3 & -1 \\ 2 & 4 \end{bmatrix} - \begin{bmatrix} 5 & -2 \\ -3 & 8 \end{bmatrix}$

35. $\begin{bmatrix} 6.1 & -4 \\ -3.7 & -2.1 \end{bmatrix} - \begin{bmatrix} 7.0 & -2.3 \\ -1.6 & 4.2 \end{bmatrix}$

36. The temperature in the evening was 68°F. The following morning, the temperature was 39°F. What is the difference between the two temperatures?

37. What is the difference in altitude between Mt. Everest, which is about 29,028 ft above sea level, and Death Valley, which is about 282 ft below sea level?

38. Suppose the balance in your checking account was $234.15 when you wrote a check for $439.87. (This is known as overdrawing your account.) Describe the account's new balance.

39. After three plays in which a football team lost 7 yd, gained 3 yd, and lost 1 yd, respectively, the ball was placed on the team's own 30-yd line. Where was the ball before the three plays?

Practice 1-6

Multiplying and Dividing Real Numbers

Simplify each expression.

$(-3)(-3)(-3)(-3)$
$-9 \quad -9$

1. $(-2)(8)$
-16

2. $(-6)(-9)$
-54

3. $(-3)^4$
-81

4. -2^5 $(-2)(-2)(-2)(-2)(-2)$
$-32 \quad -2 \quad -4 \quad -4$

5. $(6)(-8)$
-48

6. $(-14)^2$
-28

7. $2(-4)(-6)$
70

8. $-30 \div (-5)$

9. $\dfrac{-52}{-13}$

10. $(-8)(5)(-3)$

11. -7^2
-14

12. -3^5 $(-3)(-3)(-3)(-3)(-3)$
$-135 \quad -9 \quad -9$

13. $\dfrac{-68}{17}$

14. $\dfrac{(-4)(-13)}{-26}$

15. $\dfrac{225}{(-3)(-5)}$

Evaluate each expression.

16. x^3 for $x = -5$
-15

17. $s^2 t \div 10$ for $s = -2$ and $t = 10$

18. $-2m + 4n^2$ for $m = -6$ and $n = -5$

19. $\dfrac{v}{w}$ for $v = \dfrac{2}{5}$ and $w = -\dfrac{1}{2}$

20. $-cd^2$ for $c = 2$ and $d = -4$

21. $(x + 4)^2$ for $x = -11$

22. $\left(\dfrac{a}{b}\right)^2 + b^3$ for $a = 24$ and $b = -6$

23. $4p^2 + 7q^3$ for $p = -3$ and $q = -2$

24. $(e + f)^4$ for $e = -3$ and $f = 7$

25. $5f^2 - z^2$ for $f = -1$ and $z = -4$

Simplify each expression.

26. $2^4 - 3^2 + 5^2$

27. $(-8)^2 - 4^3$

28. $32 \div (-7 + 5)^3$

29. $\dfrac{3}{4} \div \left(-\dfrac{3}{7}\right)$

30. $18 + 4^2 \div (-8)$

31. $26 \div [4 - (-9)]$

32. $4^3 - (2 - 5)^3$

33. $-(-4)^3$

34. $(-8)(-5)(-3)$

35. $(-3)^2 - 4^2$

36. $\dfrac{-45}{-15}$

37. $(-2)^6$
-12

38. $\dfrac{-90}{6}$

39. $\dfrac{-15}{(7 - 4)}$

40. $\dfrac{195}{-13}$

Evaluate each expression.

41. $(a + b)^2$ for $a = 6$ and $b = -8$

42. $d^3 \div e$ for $d = -6$ and $e = -3$

43. $(m + 5n)^3$ for $m = 2$ and $n = -1$

44. $j^5 - 5k$ for $j = -4$ and $k = -1$

45. $xy + z$ for $x = -4, y = 3$, and $z = -3$

46. $4s \div (-3t)$ for $s = -6$ and $t = -2$

47. $\dfrac{r^3}{s}$ for $r = -6$ and $s = -2$

48. $\dfrac{-h^5}{-4}$ for $h = 4$

Name _____ Class _____ Date _____

Practice 1-7

The Distributive Property

Simplify each expression.

1. $2(x + 6)$

2. $-5(8 - b)$

3. $4(-x + 7)$

4. $(5c - 7)(-3)$

5. $-2.5(3a + 5)$

6. $-(3k - 12)$

7. $-\frac{3}{4}(12 - 16d)$

8. $\frac{2}{3}(6h - 1)$

9. $(-3.2x + 2.1)(-6)$

10. $3.5(3x - 8)$

11. $4(x + 7)$

12. $-2.5(2a - 4)$

13. $\frac{2}{3}(12 - 15d)$

14. $-2(k - 11)$

15. $-\frac{1}{3}(6h + 15)$

16. $(2c - 8)(-4)$

17. $-(4 - 2b)$

18. $2(3x - 9)$

19. $4(2r + 8)$

20. $-5(b - 5)$

21. $3(f + 2)$

22. $6h + 5(h - 5)$

23. $-5d + 3(2d - 7)$

24. $7 + 2(4x - 3)$

25. $2(3h + 2) - 4h$

26. $2(4 + y)$

27. $\frac{1}{2}(2n - 4) - 2n$

28. $-w + 4(w + 3)$

29. $0.4(3d - 5)$

30. $-4d + 2(3 + d)$

31. $2x + \frac{3}{4}(4x + 16)$

32. $2(3a + 2)$

33. $5(t - 3) - 2t$

34. $5(b + 4) - 6b$

35. $\frac{2}{5}(5k + 35) - 8$

36. $0.4(2s + 4)$

37. $\frac{2}{3}(9b - 27)$

38. $\frac{1}{2}(12n - 8)$

39. $0.5(2x - 4)$

40. $2(a - 4) + 15$

41. $13 + 2(5c - 2)$

42. $7 + 2(\frac{1}{5}a - 3)$

43. $5(3x + 12)$

44. $2(m + 1)$

45. $4(2a + 2) - 17$

46. $-4x + 3(2x - 5)$

47. $3(t - 12)$

48. $-6 - 3(2k + 4)$

Write an expression for each phrase.

49. 5 times the quantity x plus 6

50. twice the quantity y minus 8

51. the product of -15 and the quantity x minus 5

52. 32 divided by the quantity y plus 12

53. -8 times the quantity 4 decreased by w

54. the quantity x plus 9 times the quantity 7 minus x

Practice 1-8

Name the property that each equation illustrates.

1. $83 + 6 = 6 + 83$

2. $8 + x = x + 8$

3. $1 \cdot 4y = 4y$

4. $15x + 15y = 15(x + y)$

5. $(8 \cdot 7) \cdot 6 = 8 \cdot (7 \cdot 6)$

6. $\frac{2}{3}\left(\frac{3}{2}\right) = 1$

7. $3(a + 2b) = 3a + 6b$

8. $7x + 2y = 2y + 7x$

9. $7 + (8 + 15) = (7 + 8) + 15$

10. $x + (-x) = 0$

11. $x + y = y + x$

12. $6 \cdot (x \cdot y) = (6 \cdot x) \cdot y$

13. $16 + 0 = 16$

14. $3w + 5y = 5y + 3w$

15. $7(3 + 4y) = 21 + 28y$

16. $0 = 30 \cdot 0$

17. $4a + (5b + 6c) = (4a + 5b) + 6c$

18. $ab + c = ba + c$

19. $wr = rw$

20. $20(a + b) = 20(b + a)$

Give a reason to justify each step.

21. a. $4c + 3(2 + c) = 4c + 6 + 3c$
   b. $\qquad\qquad\quad = 4c + 3c + 6$
   c. $\qquad\qquad\quad = (4c + 3c) + 6$
   d. $\qquad\qquad\quad = (4 + 3)c + 6$
   e. $\qquad\qquad\quad = 7c + 6$

22. a. $8w - 4(7 - w) = 8w - 28 + 4w$
   b. $\qquad\qquad\quad = 8w + (-28) + 4w$
   c. $\qquad\qquad\quad = 8w + 4w + (-28)$
   d. $\qquad\qquad\quad = (8 + 4)w + (-28)$
   e. $\qquad\qquad\quad = 12w + (-28)$
   f. $\qquad\qquad\quad = 12w - 28$

23. a. $5(x + y) + 2(x + y) = 5x + 5y + 2x + 2y$
   b. $\qquad\qquad\qquad\quad = 5x + 2x + 5y + 2y$
   c. $\qquad\qquad\qquad\quad = (5 + 2)x + (5 + 2)y$
   d. $\qquad\qquad\qquad\quad = 7x + 7y$

Use mental math to simplify each expression.

24. $48 + 27 + 2 + 3$

25. $10 \cdot 72 \cdot 5 \cdot 2$

26. $10 \cdot 8 \cdot 3 \cdot 10$

27. $8\frac{1}{2} + 4\frac{1}{3} + 2\frac{1}{2} + 2\frac{2}{3}$

28. Henry bought an apple for $0.75, some apricots for $1.50, some cherries for $3.25, and three bananas for $1.50. Find the total cost of the fruit.

29. Suppose you buy some camping supplies. You purchase waterproof matches for $3.95, a compass for $18.25, flashlight batteries for $3.75, and a map for $2.05. Find the total cost of the supplies.

30. You go to the video store and rent some DVDs for $8.50 and a video game for $3.69. While there, you buy a box of popcorn for $2.31 and a candy bar for $1.50. Find the total cost of the items.

Name_____ Class_____ Date_____

Practice 1-9

Graphing Data on the Coordinate Plane

Name the coordinates of each point on the graph at the right.

1. A   **2.** B

3. C   **4.** D

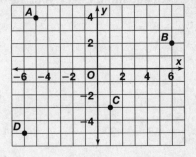

In which quadrant would you find each point?

5. $(-3, 4)$ **6.** $(-6, -6)$

7. $(1, 5)$ **8.** $(8, -9)$

Use the data in each table to draw a scatter plot.

9. Height and Hourly Pay of Ten People

Height (inches)	Hourly Pay	Height (inches)	Hourly Pay
62	$6.00	72	$8.00
65	$8.50	72	$6.00
68	$6.50	73	$7.50
70	$6.00	74	$6.25
70	$7.50	74	$8.00

10. Speed of Winds in Some U.S. Cities

Station	Average Speed (mi/h)	Highest Speed (mi/h)
Atlanta, GA	9.1	60
Casper, WY	12.9	81
Dallas, TX	10.7	73
Mobile, AL	9.0	63
St. Louis, MO	9.7	60

Source: National Climatic Data Center

11. In Exercise 9, is there a *positive correlation*, a *negative correlation*, or *no correlation* between height and hourly pay?

12. In Exercise 10, is there a *positive correlation*, a *negative correlation*, or *no correlation* between average wind speed and highest wind speed?

Would you expect a *positive correlation*, a *negative correlation*, or *no correlation* between the two data sets? Why?

13. a person's age and the number of pets he or she has

14. the number of times you brush your teeth and the number of cavities you get

15. the number of days it rains per year and the number of umbrellas sold

Is there a *positive correlation*, a *negative correlation*, or *no correlation* between the two data sets in each scatter plot?

16. 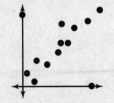   **17.** 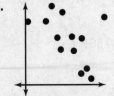   **18.**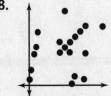

Algebra 1 Chapter 1   Lesson 1-9 Practice   **9**

© Pearson Education, Inc. All rights reserved.

Practice 2-1

Solving One-Step Equations

Solve each equation. Check your answer.

1. $g - 6 = 2$

2. $15 + b = 4$

3 $8 = h + 24$

4. $63 = 7x$

5. $x + 7 = 17$

6. $-2n = -46$

7. $\frac{c}{14} = -3$

8. $\frac{x}{2} = 13$

9. $\frac{a}{5} = 3$

10. $r - 63 = -37$

11. $5 + d = 27$

12. $2b = -16$

13. $4y = 48$

14. $c - 25 = 19$

15. $a + 4 = 9.6$

16. $x + 29 = 13$

17. $-3d = -63$

18. $3f = -21.6$

19. $-\frac{x}{8} = 12$

20. $a - \frac{1}{3} = \frac{2}{3}$

21. $n - 3 = -3$

Write an equation to model each situation. Then solve.

22. A stack of 12 bricks is 27 in. high. What is the height of each brick?

23. The sum of Juanita's age and Sara's age is 33 yr. If Sara is 15 years old, how old is Juanita?

24. The tallest player on the basketball team is $77\frac{3}{4}$ in. tall. This is $9\frac{1}{2}$ in. taller than the shortest player. How tall is the shortest player?

25. The equatorial diameter of Jupiter is about 89,000 mi. This is about 11.23 times the equatorial diameter of Earth. What is the equatorial diameter of Earth? Round to the nearest integer.

26. The distance from Baltimore to New York is about 171 mi. This is about 189 mi less than the distance from Baltimore to Boston. How far is Baltimore from Boston if you stop in New York along the way?

Solve each equation. Check your answer.

27. $y - 8 = -15$

28. $a + 27.7 = -36.6$

29. $3x = 27$

30. $a + 5 = -19$

31. $m - 9.5 = -27.4$

32. $-54 = -6s$

33. $x + \frac{1}{3} = \frac{5}{6}$

34. $-\frac{s}{3} = 7$

35. $\frac{m}{12} = -4.2$

36. $\frac{a}{3} = -11$

37. $-\frac{z}{8} = -3.7$

38. $-\frac{y}{11} = -6.1$

39. $-17.5 = 2.5d$

40. $b - 48 = -29$

41. $96 = -3h$

42. $-4.2x = 15.96$

43. $x + 87.8 = 38.1$

44. $-5x = 85$

45. $-\frac{x}{5} = 4.8$

46. $d + \frac{2}{3} = -\frac{1}{2}$

47. $-\frac{t}{2} = -9$

48. $45.6 = 6x$

49. $19.5 = -39.5 + f$

50. $m - 21 = -43$

Practice 2-2

Solve each equation. Check your answer.

1. $5a + 2 = 7$ **2.** $2x + 3 = 7$ **3.** $3b + 6 = 12$

4. $9 = 5 + 4t$ **5.** $4a + 1 = 13$ **6.** $-t + 2 = 12$

Write an equation to model each situation. Then solve.

7. You want to buy a bouquet of yellow roses and baby's breath for $16. The baby's breath costs $3.50 per bunch, and the roses cost $2.50 each. You want one bunch of baby's breath and some roses for your bouquet. How many roses can you buy?

8. Suppose you walk at the rate of 210 ft/min. You need to walk 10,000 ft. How many more minutes will it take you to finish if you have already walked 550 ft?

9. Suppose you have shelled 6.5 lb of pecans, and you can shell pecans at a rate of 1.5 lb per hour. How many more hours will it take you to shell a total of 11 lb of pecans?

10. To mail a first class letter, the U.S. Postal Service charges $.34 for the first ounce and $.21 for each additional ounce. It costs $1.18 to mail your letter. How many ounces does your letter weigh?

11. Suppose you want to buy one pair of pants and several pairs of socks. The pants cost $24.95, and the socks are $5.95 per pair. How many pairs of socks can you buy if you have $50.00 to spend?

Solve each equation. Check your answer.

12. $5.8n + 3.7 = 29.8$ **13.** $67 = -3y + 16$ **14.** $-d + 7 = 3$

15. $\frac{m}{9} + 7 = 3$ **16.** $6.78 + 5.2x = -36.9$ **17.** $5z + 9 = -21$

18. $3x - 7 = 35$ **19.** $36.9 = 3.7b - 14.9$ **20.** $4s - 13 = 51$

21. $9f + 16 = 70$ **22.** $11.6 + 3a = -16.9$ **23.** $-9 = -\frac{h}{12} + 5$

24. $-c + 2 = 5$ **25.** $-67 = -8n + 5$ **26.** $22 = 7 - 3a$

27. $\frac{k}{3} - 19 = -26$ **28.** $-21 = \frac{n}{3} + 2$ **29.** $3x + 5.7 = 15$

30. $\frac{a}{5} - 2 = -13$ **31.** $2x + 23 = 49$ **32.** $\frac{x}{2} + 8 = -3$

Justify each step.

33. $24 - x = -16$
a. $24 - x - 24 = -16 - 24$
b. $-x = -40$
c. $-1(-x) = -1(-40)$
d. $x = 40$

34. $\frac{x}{7} + 4 = 15$
a. $\frac{x}{7} + 4 - 4 = 15 - 4$
b. $\frac{x}{7} = 11$
c. $7(\frac{x}{7}) = 7(11)$
d. $x = 77$

35. $-8 = 2x - 5$
a. $-8 + 5 = 2x - 5 + 5$
b. $-3 = 2x$
c. $-\frac{3}{2} = \frac{2x}{2}$
d. $-\frac{3}{2} = x$

Practice 2-3

Solving Multi-Step Equations

Solve each equation. Check your answer.

1. $2n + 3n + 7 = -41$

2. $2x - 5x + 6.3 = -14.4$

3. $2z + 9.75 - 7z = -5.15$

4. $3h - 5h + 11 = 17$

5. $2t + 8 - t = -3$

6. $6a - 2a = -36$

7. $3c - 8c + 7 = -18$

8. $7g + 14 - 5g = -8$

9. $2b - 6 + 3b = 14$

10. $2(a - 4) + 15 = 13$

11. $7 + 2(a - 3) = -9$

12. $13 + 2(5c - 2) = 29$

13. $5(3x + 12) = -15$

14. $4(2a + 2) - 17 = 15$

15. $2(m + 1) = 16$

16. $-4x + 3(2x - 5) = 31$

17. $-6 - 3(2k + 4) = 18$

18. $3(t - 12) = 27$

19. $-w + 4(w + 3) = -12$

20. $4 = 0.4(3d - 5)$

21. $-4d + 2(3 + d) = -14$

22. $2x + \frac{3}{4}(4x + 16) = 7$

23. $2(3a + 2) = -8$

24. $5(t - 3) - 2t = -30$

25. $5(b + 4) - 6b = -24$

26. $\frac{2}{5}(5k + 35) - 8 = 12$

27. $0.4(2s + 4) = 4.8$

28. $\frac{2}{3}(9b - 27) = 36$

29. $\frac{1}{2}(12n - 8) = 26$

30. $0.5(2x - 4) = -17$

31. $18 = \frac{c + 5}{2}$

32. $\frac{2}{9}s = -6$

33. $\frac{1}{3}x = \frac{1}{2}$

34. $\frac{2}{3}g + \frac{1}{2}g = 14$

35. $\frac{3x + 7}{2} = 8$

36. $\frac{2x - 6}{4} = -7$

37. $\frac{2}{3}k + \frac{1}{4}k = 22$

38. $-\frac{4}{7}h = -28$

39. $-8 = \frac{4}{5}k$

40. $\frac{3}{4} - \frac{1}{3}z = \frac{1}{4}$

41. $-9 = \frac{3}{4}m$

42. $\frac{5}{6}c - \frac{2}{3}c = \frac{1}{3}$

43. $\frac{4}{5} = -\frac{4}{7}g$

44. $\frac{9x + 6 - 4x}{2} = 8$

45. $-\frac{1}{6}d = -4$

Write an equation to model each situation. Then solve.

46. The attendance at a baseball game was 400 people. Student tickets cost $2 and adult tickets cost $3. Total ticket sales were $1050. How many tickets of each type were sold?

47. The perimeter of a pool table is 30 ft. The table is twice as long as it is wide. What is the length of the pool table?

48. Lopez spent $\frac{1}{3}$ of his vacation money for travel and $\frac{2}{5}$ of his vacation money for lodging. He spent $1100 for travel and lodging. What is the total amount of money he spent on his vacation?

49. Victoria weighs $\frac{5}{7}$ as much as Mario. Victoria weighs 125 lb. How much does Mario weigh?

50. Denise's cell phone plan is $29.95 per month plus $.10 per minute for each minute over 300 minutes of call time. Denise's cell phone bill is $99.95. For how many minutes was she billed?

Practice 2-4

Equations with Variables on Both Sides

Solve each equation. Check your answer. If appropriate, write *identity* or *no solution.*

1. $7 - 2n = n - 14$

2. $2(4 - 2r) = -2(r + 5)$

3. $3d + 8 = 2d - 7$

4. $6t = 3(t + 4) - t$

5. $8z - 7 = 3z - 7 + 5z$

6. $7x - 8 = 3x + 12$

7. $3(n - 1) = 5n + 3 - 2n$

8. $2(6 - 4d) = 25 - 9d$

9. $4s - 12 = -5s + 51$

10. $8(2f - 3) = 4(4f - 8)$

11. $6k - 25 = 7 - 2k$

12. $3v - 9 = 7 + 2v - v$

13. $4(b - 1) = -4 + 4b$

14. $\frac{1}{4}x + \frac{1}{2} = \frac{1}{4}x - \frac{1}{2}$

15. $6 - 4d = 16 - 9d$

16. $\frac{2}{3}a - \frac{3}{4} = \frac{3}{4}a$

17. $2s - 12 + 2s = 4s - 12$

18. $3.6y = 5.4 + 3.3y$

19. $4.3v - 6 = 8 + 2.3v$

20. $4b - 1 = -4 + 4b + 3$

21. $\frac{2}{3}(6x + 3) = 4x + 2$

22. $6y + 9 = 3(2y + 3)$

23. $4g + 7 = 5g - 1 - g$

24. $2(n + 2) = 5n - 5$

25. $6 - 3d = 5(2 - d)$

26. $6.1h = 9.3 - 3.2h$

27. $-4.4s - 2 = -5.5s - 4.2$

28. $3(2f + 4) = 2(3f - 6)$

29. $\frac{3}{4}t - \frac{5}{6} = \frac{2}{3}t$

30. $3v + 8 = 8 + 2v + v$

31. $\frac{1}{2}d - \frac{3}{4} = \frac{3}{5}d$

32. $5(r + 3) = 2r + 6$

33. $8 - 3(p - 4) = 2p$

Write an equation to model each situation. Then solve. Check your answer.

34. Hans needs to rent a moving truck. Suppose Company A charges a rate of $40 per day and Company B charges a $60 fee plus $20 per day. For what number of days is the cost the same?

35. Suppose a video store charges nonmembers $4 to rent each video. A store membership costs $21 and members pay only $2.50 to rent each video. For what number of videos is the cost the same?

36. Suppose your club is selling candles to raise money. It costs $100 to rent a booth from which to sell the candles. If the candles cost your club $1 each and are sold for $5 each, how many candles must be sold to equal your expenses?

Find the value of *x.*

37.

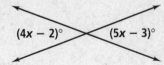

$(4x - 2)°$ $(5x - 3)°$

38.

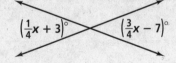

$\left(\frac{1}{4}x + 3\right)°$ $\left(\frac{3}{4}x - 7\right)°$

39.

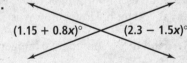

$(1.15 + 0.8x)°$ $(2.3 - 1.5x)°$

Practice 2-5

Equations and Problem Solving

Write and solve an equation for each situation.

1. A passenger train's speed is 60 mi/h, and a freight train's speed is 40 mi/h. The passenger train travels the same distance in 1.5 h less time than the freight train. How long does each train take to make the trip?

2. Lois rode her bike to visit a friend. She traveled at 10 mi/h. While she was there, it began to rain. Her friend drove her home in a car traveling at 25 mi/h. Lois took 1.5 h longer to go to her friend's than to return home. How many hours did it take Lois to ride to her friend's house?

3. May rides her bike the same distance that Leah walks. May rides her bike 10 km/h faster than Leah walks. If it takes May 1 h and Leah 3 h to travel that distance, how fast does each travel?

4. The length of a rectangle is 4 in. greater than the width. The perimeter of the rectangle is 24 in. Find the dimensions of the rectangle.

5. The length of a rectangle is twice the width. The perimeter is 48 in. Find the dimensions of the rectangle.

6. At 10:00 A.M., a car leaves a house at a rate of 60 mi/h. At the same time, another car leaves the same house at a rate of 50 mi/h in the opposite direction. At what time will the cars be 330 miles apart?

7. Marla begins walking at 3 mi/h toward the library. Her friend meets her at the halfway point and drives her the rest of the way to the library. The distance to the library is 4 miles. How many hours did Marla walk?

8. Fred begins walking toward John's house at 3 mi/h. John leaves his house at the same time and walks toward Fred's house on the same path at a rate of 2 mi/h. How long will it be before they meet if the distance between the houses is 4 miles?

9. A train leaves the station at 6:00 P.M. traveling west at 80 mi/h. On a parallel track, a second train leaves the station 3 hours later traveling west at 100 mi/h. At what time will the second train catch up with the first?

10. It takes 1 hour longer to fly to St. Paul at 200 mi/h than it does to return at 250 mi/h. How far away is St. Paul?

11. Find three consecutive integers whose sum is 126.

12. The sum of four consecutive odd integers is 216. Find the four integers.

13. A rectangular picture frame is to be 8 in. longer than it is wide. Dennis uses 84 in. of oak to frame the picture. What is the width of the frame?

14. Each of two congruent sides of an isosceles triangle is 8 in. less than twice the base. The perimeter of the triangle is 74 in. What is the length of the base?

Practice 2-6

Formulas

Solve each formula in terms of the given variable.

1. $ad = f$; a **2.** $n + 3 = q$; n **3.** $2(j + k) = m$; k **4.** $2s + t = r$; t

5. $m + 2n = p$; n **6.** $\frac{2}{w} = \frac{x}{5}$; w **7.** $5a - b = 7$; a **8.** $h = \frac{p}{n}$; p

9. $5d - 2g = 9$; g **10.** $x + 3y = z$; x **11.** $y = mx + b$; x **12.** $V = \ell wh$; ℓ

The formula $A = 2h(\ell + w)$ gives the lateral area A of a rectangular solid with length ℓ, width w, and height h.

13. Solve this formula for h.   **14.** Find h if $A = 144$ cm^2, $\ell = 7$ cm, and $w = 5$ cm.

15. Solve this formula for ℓ.   **16.** Find ℓ if $A = 729.8$ in.^{2}, $h = 17.8$ in., and $w = 6.4$ in.

17. Find h if $A = 37.4$ ft^2, $\ell = 4.3$ ft, and $w = 6.7$ ft.

18. Find ℓ if $A = 9338$ m^2, $h = 29$ m, and $w = 52$ m.

The formula $P = \frac{F}{A}$ gives the pressure P for a force F and an area A.

19. Solve this formula for A.   **20.** Find A if $P = 14.8$ lb/in.^{2} and $F = 2960$ lb.

21. Solve this formula for F.   **22.** Find F if $P = 240$ lb/in.^{2} and $A = 20$ in.^{2}.

23. Find A if $P = 46.8$ lb/in.^{2} and $F = 2340$ lb.   **24.** Find F if $P = 24.5$ lb/in.^{2} and $A = 33.8$ in.^{2}.

Solve each formula in terms of the given variable.

25. $3n - t = s$; t **26.** $\frac{b + 3}{e} = \frac{f}{2}$; e **27.** $w = 2xyz$; y **28.** $k = 3mh + 3$; h

29. $ab = 6 + cd$; a **30.** $2a + 4b = d$; b **31.** $4xy + 3 = 5z$; y **32.** $-2(3a - b) = c$; b

The formula $V = \frac{1}{3}\ell wh$ gives the volume V of a rectangular pyramid with length ℓ, width w, and height h.

33. Solve this formula for w.   **34.** Find w if $V = 64$ m^3, $\ell = 6$ m, and $h = 4$ m.

35. Solve this formula for h.   **36.** Find h if $V = 30.45$ ft^3, $\ell = 6.3$ ft, and $w = 2.5$ ft.

37. Find w if $V = 2346$ in.^{3}, $\ell = 17$ in., and $h = 18$ in.   **38.** Find h if $V = 7$ ft^3, $\ell = \frac{7}{4}$ ft, and $w = \frac{3}{4}$ ft.

Solve each formula in terms of the given variable.

39. $2m - 3p = 1$; p **40.** $a = b + cd$; b **41.** $a + b = 2xz$; z **42.** $x = 2y + 3z$; y

43. $\frac{a}{b} = \frac{c}{d}$; d **44.** $2ab + 4 = d$; a **45.** $\frac{5}{2} = \frac{1}{2}(b - c)$; b **46.** $d(a - b) = c$; a

Practice 2-7

Find the mean, median, mode, and range.

1. number of cars sold in the past 10 days
   1 5 3 2 1 0 4 2 6 1

2. utility bills for the past 6 months
   $90 $120 $140 $135 $112 $126

3. prices of a sweater in 5 different stores
   $31.25 $27.50 $28.00 $36.95 $32.10

4. scores on a 10-point quiz
   7 9 10 8 4 2 6 10 8

5. hourly wages
   $7.25 $6.75 $8.10 $9.56 $7.10 $7.75

6. ages of students on the quiz team
   15 15 14 16 17 16 16 15

Write and solve an equation to find the value of x.

7. 4.8, 1.6, 5.2, x; mean 3.7

8. 40, 98, 94, 102, 21, x; mean 88

9. 100, 172, 85, 92, x; mean 115

10. 25.6, 19.3, 19, x, mean 24

11. In his eight games against Boston, a baseball pitcher threw the following number of strikeouts: 1, 2, 4, 2, 1, 3, 3, and 0. In his five games against St. Louis, he recorded strikeouts as follows: 3, 1, 2, 3, and 2. Did the pitcher average more strikeouts against Boston or against St. Louis?

12. Randy had grades of 85, 92, 96, and 89 on his last four math tests. What grade does he need on his next test to have an average of 92?

13. To test the exhaust fumes of a car, an inspector took six samples. The exhaust samples contained the following amounts of gas in parts per million (ppm): 8, 5, 7, 6, 9, and 5. If the maximum allowable mean is 6 ppm, did the car pass the test? Explain.

14. A coffee machine is considered reliable if the range of amounts of coffee that it dispenses is less than 2 fluid ounces (fl oz). In eight tries, a particular machine dispensed the following amounts: 7.1, 6.8, 7.6, 7.1, 7.4, 6.8, 7, and 6.7 fl oz. Is the machine reliable? Explain.

15. According to its producer, an off-Broadway show would make a profit if an average of at least 1100 tickets were sold per show. For the past 12 shows, the number of tickets sold was as follows: 1000, 800, 1600, 900, 1200, 900, 800, 1700, 900, 1200, 1000, and 1200. Using the mean as the average, did the show make a profit for these 12 shows?

16. a. A bakery collected the following data about the number of loaves of fresh bread sold on each of 24 business days. Make a stem-and-leaf plot for the data.

43	39	17	38	50	42	34	28	37	42	40	33
72	36	45	21	29	44	41	37	40	35	51	54

   b. Find the mean, median, mode, and range of the data.

17. a. The following numbers of calls were made to the police department in the last 24 days. Make a stem-and-leaf plot for the data.

32	42	35	52	58	52	46	61	52	63	81	61
63	39	41	48	62	61	58	34	49	47	49	31

   b. Find the mean, median, mode, and range of the data.

Name _____ Class _____ Date _____

Practice 3-1

Inequalities and Their Graphs

Determine whether each number is a solution of the given inequality.

1. $x \leq -8$ **a.** -10 **b.** 6 **c.** -8

2. $-1 > x$ **a.** 0 **b.** -3 **c.** -6

3. $w < \frac{18}{7}$ **a.** 5 **b.** -2 **c.** $3\frac{1}{2}$

4. $0.65 \geq y$ **a.** 0.43 **b.** -0.65 **c.** 0.56

5. $2y + 1 > -5$ **a.** -4 **b.** -2 **c.** 4

6. $7x - 14 \leq 6x - 16$ **a.** 0 **b.** -4 **c.** 2

7. $n(n - 6) \geq -4$ **a.** 3 **b.** -2 **c.** 5

Write an inequality for each graph.

8.

9.

10.

11.

Write each inequality in words and then graph.

12. $x > 6$ 13. $y \leq -10$ 14. $8 \geq b$

15. $-4 < w$ 16. $x < -7$ 17. $x \geq 12$

Define a variable and write an inequality to model each situation.

18. The temperature in a refrigerated truck must be kept at or below 38°F.

19. The maximum weight on an elevator is 2000 pounds.

20. A least 20 students were sick with the flu.

21. The maximum occupancy in an auditorium is 250 people.

22. The maximum speed on the highway is 55 mi/h.

23. A student must have at least 450 out of 500 points to earn an A.

24. The circumference of an official major league baseball is at least 9.00 inches.

Match the inequality with its graph.

25. $6 < x$ 26. $-6 \geq x$ 27. $4 > x$ 28. $x \leq -4$

A.

B.

C.

D.

Practice 3-2

Solving Inequalities Using Addition and Subtraction

Solve each inequality. Graph and check the solution.

1. $n - 7 \geq 2$ **2.** $10 + y > 12$ **3.** $3.2 < r + 4.7$ **4.** $7 + b > 13$

5. $n + \frac{3}{4} > \frac{1}{2}$ **6.** $-\frac{5}{7} \geq c + \frac{2}{7}$ **7.** $g + 4.6 < 5.9$ **8.** $0 > d - 2.7$

9. $f + 4 \geq 14$ **10.** $x + 1 \leq -3$ **11.** $d - 13 \leq -8$ **12.** $m - 7 \geq -8$

13. $12 + v < 19$ **14.** $-4 \leq t + 9$ **15.** $6 < y - 3$ **16.** $a + 15 > 19$

17. $8 + d < 9$ **18.** $s + 3 \leq 3$ **19.** $9 + h \leq 5$ **20.** $7.6 \geq t - 2.4$

Write and solve an inequality that models each situation.

21. It will take at least 360 points for Kiko's team to win the math contest. The scores for Kiko's teammates were 94, 82, and 87, but one of Kiko's teammates lost 2 of those points for an incomplete answer. How many points must Kiko earn for her team to win the contest?

22. This season, Nora has 125 at-bats in softball. By the end of the season she wants to have at least 140 at-bats. How many more at-bats does Nora need to reach her goal?

23. The average wind speed increased 19 mi/h from 8 A.M. to noon. The average wind speed decreased 5 mi/h from noon to 4 P.M. At 4 P.M., the average wind speed was at least 32 mi/h. What is the minimum value of the average wind speed at 8 A.M.?

24. Suppose it takes no more than 25 min for you to get to school. If you have traveled for 13.5 min already, how much longer, at most, might you take to get to school?

25. Joan has started a physical fitness program. One of her goals is to be able to run at least 5 mi without stopping. She can now run 3.5 mi without stopping. How many more miles must she run non-stop to achieve her goal?

26. Suppose you can get a higher interest rate on your savings if you maintain a balance of at least $1000 in your savings account. The balance in your savings account is now $1058. You deposit $44.50 into your account. What is the greatest amount that you can withdraw and still get the higher interest rate?

Solve each inequality. Graph and check the solution.

27. $\frac{3}{4} + z \geq -\frac{3}{4}$ **28.** $12 + d + 3 \leq 10$ **29.** $v - \frac{3}{4} > 1\frac{1}{4}$ **30.** $8 + m > 4$

31. $2 + f > -3$ **32.** $-27 \geq w - 24$ **33.** $b + \frac{1}{2} > \frac{3}{4}$ **34.** $12 + t < 4 - 15$

35. $-14 > -16 + u$ **36.** $-7 \leq -11 + z$ **37.** $38 \geq 33 + b$ **38.** $k - 27 < -29$

39. $a + 8 \leq 10$ **40.** $b + 6 > 17$ **41.** $13 < 8 + k - 6$ **42.** $j + 1.3 > 2.8$

Practice 3-3

Solving Inequalities Using Multiplication and Division

Solve each inequality. Graph and check the solution.

1. $\frac{15}{8} \leq \frac{5}{2}s$
    2. $60 \leq 12b$
    3. $-\frac{4}{5}r < 8$
    4. $\frac{5}{2} < \frac{n}{8}$

5. $-9n \geq -36$
    6. $\frac{n}{7} \geq -6$
    7. $-7c < 28$
    8. $16d > -64$

9. $-\frac{t}{3} < -5$
    10. $54 < -6k$
    11. $\frac{w}{7} > 0$
    12. $2.6v > 6.5$

13. $-4 < -\frac{2}{5}m$
    14. $17 < \frac{p}{2}$
    15. $0.9 \leq -1.8v$
    16. $-5 \leq -\frac{x}{9}$

17. $-1 \geq \frac{d}{7}$
    18. $-3x \geq 21$
    19. $\frac{c}{12} < \frac{3}{4}$
    20. $\frac{a}{4} \leq -1$

Write and solve an inequality that models each situation.

21. Suppose you and a friend are working for a nursery planting trees. Together you can plant 8 trees per hour. What is the greatest number of hours that you and your friend would need to plant at most 40 trees?

22. Suppose the physics club is going on a field trip. Members will be riding in vans that will hold 7 people each including the driver. At least 28 people will be going on the field trip. What is the least number of vans needed to make the trip?

23. You need to buy stamps to mail some letters. The stamps cost $.34 each. What is the maximum number of stamps that you can buy with $3.84?

24. The Garcias are putting a brick border along one edge of their flower garden. The flower garden is no more than 31 ft long. If each brick is 6 in. long, what is the greatest number of bricks needed?

25. Janet needs to travel 275 mi for a conference. She needs to be at the conference in no more than 5.5 h. What is the slowest average speed that she can drive and still arrive at the conference on time?

Solve each inequality. Graph and check the solution.

26. $\frac{1}{4}h < 4.9$
    27. $\frac{7}{3}x < 21$
    28. $-\frac{1}{9}a > 9$
    29. $\frac{b}{6} \leq 2.5$

30. $-\frac{3}{5}q > 15$
    31. $84 \leq 21b$
    32. $\frac{c}{12} > -\frac{5}{6}$
    33. $80.6 \leq -6.5b$

34. $-\frac{1}{9}p > \frac{1}{3}$
    35. $-9z > 45$
    36. $\frac{1}{7}y \leq 6$
    37. $-\frac{5}{7} > -\frac{k}{14}$

38. $6.8 > \frac{y}{5}$
    39. $75 \leq 15b$
    40. $39 < -13k$
    41. $2d < 8.8$

42. $8.5v > 61.2$
    43. $-11n \geq -55$
    44. $\frac{1}{4}y < 17$
    45. $92 < -23k$

Name _____ Class _____ Date _____

Practice 3-4

Solving Multi-Step Inequalities

Solve each inequality. Graph and check the solution.

1. $2z + 7 < z + 10$

2. $4(k - 1) > 4$

3. $1.5 + 2.1y < 1.1y + 4.5$

4. $h + 2(3h + 4) \geq 1$

5. $r + 4 > 13 - 2r$

6. $6u - 18 - 4u < 22$

7. $2(3 + 3g) \geq 2g + 14$

8. $2h - 13 < -3$

9. $-4p + 28 > 8$

10. $8m - 8 \geq 12 + 4m$

11. $5 + 6a > -1$

12. $\frac{1}{2}(2t + 8) \geq 4 + 6t$

13. $-5x + 12 < -18$

14. $2(3f + 2) > 4f + 12$

15. $13t - 8t > -45$

16. $2(c - 4) \leq 10 - c$

17. $\frac{1}{2}t - \frac{1}{3}t > -1$

18. $3.4 + 1.6v < 5.9 - 0.9v$

Write and solve an inequality that models each situation.

19. Ernest works in the shipping department loading shipping crates with boxes. Each empty crate weighs 150 lb. How many boxes, each weighing 35 lb, can Ernest put in the crate if the total weight is to be no more than 850 lb?

20. Beatriz is in charge of setting up a banquet hall. She has five tables that will seat six people each. If no more than 62 people will attend, how many tables seating four people each will she need?

21. Suppose it costs $5 to enter a carnival. Each ride costs $1.25. You have $15 to spend at the carnival. What is the greatest number of rides that you can go on?

22. The cost to rent a car is $19.50 plus $.25 per mile. If you have $44 to rent a car, what is the greatest number of miles that you can drive?

23. The student council is sponsoring a concert as a fund raiser. Tickets are $3 for students and $5 for adults. The student council wants to raise at least $1000. If 200 students attend, how many adults must attend?

Solve each inequality. Check the solution.

24. $-18 < 2(12 - 3b)$

25. $5n + 3 - 4n < -5 - 3n$

26. $36 > 4(2d + 10)$

27. $2(5t - 25) + 5t < -80$

28. $3j + 2 - 2j < -10$

29. $\frac{2}{5}(5x - 15) \geq 4$

30. $7(2z + 3) > 35$

31. $2(3b - 2) < 4b + 8$

32. $\frac{1}{2}y + \frac{1}{4}y \geq -6$

33. $8(3f - 6) < -24$

34. $\frac{3}{4}k < \frac{3}{4} - \frac{1}{4}k$

35. $3(4g - 6) \geq 6(g + 2)$

36. $\frac{1}{2}(2g + 4) > -7$

37. $4(1.25y + 4.2) < 16.8$

38. $38 + 7t > -3(t + 4)$

39. $4(2d + 1) > 28$

40. $4(n - 3) < 2 - 3n$

41. $\frac{3}{4}d - \frac{1}{2} \leq 2\frac{1}{2}$

Practice 3-5

Solve each compound inequality and graph the solution.

1. $-5 < s + 5 < 5$

2. $1 < 3x + 4 < 10$

3. $k - 3 > 1$ or $k - 3 < -1$

4. $b - 2 > 18$ or $3b < 54$

5. $-4d > 8$ and $2d > -6$

6. $-4 < t + 2 < 4$

7. $-3 < 3 + s < 7$

8. $3j \geq 6$ or $3j \leq -6$

9. $-1 < \frac{1}{2}x < 1$

10. $g + 2 > -1$ or $g - 6 < -9$

11. $-6 < 9 + 3y < 6$

12. $3f > 15$ or $2f < -4$

13. $d - 3 > 4$ or $d - 3 < -4$

14. $1 > 2h + 3 > -1$

15. $7 + 2a > 9$ or $-4a > 8$

16. $2z > 2.1$ or $3z < -5.85$

17. $c - 1 \geq 2$ or $c - 1 \leq -2$

18. $h + 2.8 < 1.8$ or $h + 2.8 > 4.8$

Write and solve a compound inequality that represents each situation. Graph your solution.

19. The crowd that heard the President speak was estimated to be 10,000 people. The actual crowd could be 750 people more or less than this. What are the possible values for the actual crowd size?

20. Susie has designed an exercise program for herself. One part of the program requires her to walk between 25 and 30 miles each week. She plans to walk the same distance each day five days a week. What is the range of miles that she should walk each day?

21. A box of cereal must weigh more than 629.4 g and less than 630.6 g to pass inspection. The box in which the cereal is packaged weighs 5.5 g. What are the possible weights for the cereal?

22. Carmen works in a sporting goods store. Her goal is to sell between $500 and $600 worth of sporting equipment every week. So far this week, she has sold $395 worth of equipment. During the rest of the week, what dollar amount must Carmen sell in order to reach her goal?

Solve each compound inequality and graph the solution.

23. $2n - 1 \geq 1$ or $2n - 1 \leq -1$

24. $2k - 3 > 3$ or $2k - 3 < -3$

25. $-1 < h - 2 < 1$

26. $2.2 + p > 1$ and $1.5p < -0.3$

27. $9 < x + 2 < 11$

28. $5m + 8 < 23$ or $6m > 48$

29. $-3 \leq \frac{3}{2}x + 6 \leq 3$

30. $7 > 5 - x > 6$

31. $\frac{1}{2}x + 1 > 1$ or $\frac{1}{2}x + 1 < -1$

32. $-2 \leq s - 4 \leq 2$

33. $w - 3 > 4$ or $w - 3 < -4$

34. $6 > 4x - 2 > -6$

35. $t + 5 < 2$ or $3t + 1 > 10$

36. $2g > 12$ and $3g < 24$

37. $6x - 3 \geq 3$ or $6x - 3 \leq -3$

38. $2y - 3 > -1$ or $5 - y > 4$

Practice 3-6

Absolute Value Equations and Inequalities

Solve each inequality. Graph the solution.

1. $|d| > 2$ **2.** $|h| > 6$ **3.** $|2k| > 8$ **4.** $|s + 4| > 2$

5. $|3c - 6| \geq 3$ **6.** $|2n + 3| \leq 5$ **7.** $|3.5z| > |7|$ **8.** $\left|\frac{2}{3}x\right| \leq 4$

9. $9 > |6 + 3t|$ **10.** $|j| - 2 \geq 6$ **11.** $5 > |v + 2| + 3$ **12.** $|4y + 11| < 7$

13. $|2n - 1| \geq 1$ **14.** $\left|\frac{1}{2}x + 1\right| > 1$ **15.** $-2|h - 2| > -2$ **16.** $3|2x| \leq 12$

17. $3|s - 4| + 21 \leq 27$ **18.** $-6|w - 3| < -24$ **19.** $-\frac{1}{2}|6x - 3| \leq -\frac{3}{2}$ **20.** $-2|3j| - 8 \leq -20$

Solve each equation. If there is no solution, write *no solution*.

21. $|a| = 9.5$ **22.** $|b| = -2$ **23.** $|d| - 25 = -13$ **24.** $|6z| + 3 = 21$

25. $|3c| - 45 = -18$ **26.** $-2 = -\frac{|z|}{7}$ **27.** $|x| = -0.8$ **28.** $-4|7 + d| = -44$

Write and solve an absolute value equation or inequality that represents each situation.

29. The average number of cucumber seeds in a package is 25. The number of seeds in the package can vary by three. Find the range of acceptable numbers of seeds in each package.

30. The mean distance of the earth from the sun is 93 million miles. The distance varies by 1.6 million miles. Find the range of distances of the earth from the sun.

31. Leona was in a golf tournament last week. All four of her rounds of golf were within 2 strokes of par. If par was 72, find the range of scores that Leona could have shot for each round of the golf tournament.

32. Victor's goal is to earn $75 per week at his after-school job. Last month he was within $6.50 of his goal. Find the range of amounts that Victor might have earned last month.

33. Members of the track team can run 400 m in an average time of 58.2 s. The fastest and slowest times vary from the average by 6.4 s. Find the range of times for the track team.

34. The ideal length of a particular metal rod is 25.5 cm. The measured length may vary from the ideal length by at most 0.025 cm. Find the range of acceptable lengths for the rod.

35. When measured on a particular scale, the weight of an object may vary from its actual weight by at most 0.4 lb. If the reading on the scale is 125.2 lb, find the range of actual weights of the object.

36. One poll reported that the approval rating of the job performance of the President of the United States was 63%. The poll was said to be accurate to within 3.8%. What is the range of actual approval ratings?

Practice 4-1

Ratio and Proportion

Find each unit rate.

1. $60 for 8 h

2. $\dfrac{\$3}{4\ \text{lb}}$

3. $\dfrac{861\ \text{bagels}}{3\ \text{d}}$

4. $\dfrac{850\ \text{cal}}{1.25\ \text{h}}$

5. An 8-ounce bottle of lotion costs $4.50. What is the cost per ounce?

6. A pound of coffee costs $14.99. What is the cost per ounce?

Which pairs of ratios could form a proportion? Justify your answer.

7. $\dfrac{10}{24}, \dfrac{7}{18}$

8. $\dfrac{6}{9}, \dfrac{10}{15}$

9. $\dfrac{3}{4}, \dfrac{18}{24}$

10. $\dfrac{16}{2}, \dfrac{8}{1}$

11. $-\dfrac{4.8}{4}, -\dfrac{6.4}{5}$

Solve each proportion.

12. $\dfrac{g}{5} = \dfrac{6}{10}$

13. $\dfrac{z}{4} = \dfrac{7}{8}$

14. $\dfrac{13.2}{6} = \dfrac{m}{12}$

15. $-\dfrac{m}{5} = -\dfrac{2}{5}$

16. $\dfrac{5.5}{11} = \dfrac{x}{5}$

17. $-\dfrac{2}{3} = -\dfrac{10}{t}$

18. $\dfrac{4}{6} = \dfrac{x}{24}$

19. $\dfrac{s}{3} = \dfrac{7}{10}$

20. $\dfrac{4}{9} = \dfrac{10}{r}$

21. $\dfrac{x}{4.8} = \dfrac{6}{3.2}$

22. $\dfrac{5}{4} = \dfrac{c}{12}$

23. $-\dfrac{32}{h} = -\dfrac{1}{3}$

24. $\dfrac{2}{6} = \dfrac{p}{9}$

25. $\dfrac{f}{6} = \dfrac{3}{4}$

26. $\dfrac{15}{a} = \dfrac{3}{8}$

27. $\dfrac{3}{4} = \dfrac{k}{24}$

28. $\dfrac{a}{6} = \dfrac{3}{9}$

29. $\dfrac{4}{5} = \dfrac{k}{9}$

30. $\dfrac{3}{y} = \dfrac{5}{8}$

31. $\dfrac{t}{7} = \dfrac{9}{21}$

32. $\dfrac{2}{9} = \dfrac{10}{x}$

33. $\dfrac{x}{15} = \dfrac{3}{4}$

34. $\dfrac{18}{11} = \dfrac{49.5}{x}$

35. $\dfrac{2}{1.2} = \dfrac{5}{x}$

36. $-\dfrac{x-1}{4} = \dfrac{2}{3}$

37. $\dfrac{3}{6} = \dfrac{x-3}{8}$

38. $\dfrac{2x-2}{14} = \dfrac{2x-4}{6}$

39. $\dfrac{x+2}{x-2} = \dfrac{4}{8}$

40. $\dfrac{x+2}{6} = \dfrac{x-1}{12}$

41. $-\dfrac{x+8}{10} = -\dfrac{x-3}{2}$

42. You are riding your bicycle. It takes you 28 min to go 8 mi. If you continue traveling at the same rate, how long will it take you to go 15 mi?

43. Suppose you traveled 84 mi in 1.5 h. Moving at the same speed, how many mi would you cover in $3\frac{1}{4}$ h?

44. A canary's heart beats 130 times in 12 s. Use a proportion to find how many times its heart beats in 50 s.

45. Your car averages 18 mi per gal on the highway. If gas costs $1.85 per gal, how much does it cost in dollars per mi to drive your car on the highway?

Practice 4-2

Proportions and Similar Figures

Each pair of figures is similar. Find the length of *x*.

1.
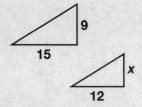

2.
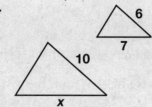

3.
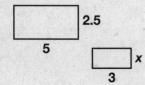

4.
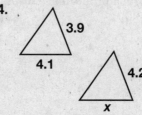

5.
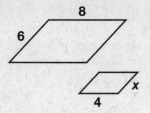

6.
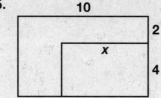

7.
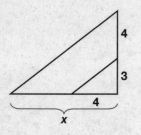

8.
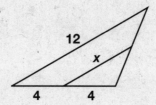

Use a proportion to solve.

9. △ABC is similar to △XYZ. The length AB is 10. The length BC is 7. Find the length XY if the length YZ is 14.

10. Marty has a scale model of a car. The scale is 1 in. : 32 in. If the model is 6.75 in. long, how long is the actual car?

11. A blueprint scale is 1 in. : 12 ft. The width of a building is 48 ft. What is the width of the building on the blueprint?

12. Angie is using similar triangles to find the height of a tree. A stick that is 5 ft tall casts a shadow that is 4 ft long. The tree casts a shadow that is 22 ft long. How tall is the tree?

13. △ABC is similar to △XYZ. The length AC is 10. The length BC is 16. What is the length XZ if the length YZ is 12?

14. A map has a scale of 1 in. : 25 mi. Two cities are 175 mi apart. How far apart are they on the map?

Practice 4-3

Solve each problem.

1. 25% of what is 28? **2.** What percent of 72 is 18? **3.** 60% of what is 45?

4. What percent of 12 is 6? **5.** What is 60% of 12? **6.** 75% of what is 48?

7. What is 20% of 650? **8.** What percent of 150 is 90? **9.** What percent of 90 is 63?

10. What is 38% of 60? **11.** 22.5% of what is 42? **12.** 45% of what is 99?

13. What percent of 210 is 10.5? **14.** 160% of what is 124? **15.** What is 39% of 1500?

16. What is 250% of 14? **17.** What percent of 20 is 36? **18.** What is 8.25% of 160?

Write an equation to model each question and solve.

19. Pablo has a goal to lose 25 lb. He has lost 16 lb. What percent of his goal has he reached?

20. You spent 16% of your vacation money on food. If you spent $48 on food, how much money did you spend on your vacation?

21. A writer earns $3400 a month. Last month she spent $204 on food. What percent of her income was spent on food?

22. Kiko spends 30% of her monthly income on rent. If she pays $810 for rent each month, what is her monthly income?

23. Suppose that 62.5% of freshmen entering a college graduate from it. If there are 2680 freshmen, how many will graduate from that college?

The formula for determining simple interest is $I = prt$. Using this formula, solve the following problems.

24. You invest $1500 for three years. Find the amount of simple interest you earn at an annual rate of 8.25%.

25. Suppose you invested $1200 for four years. You earned $312 in simple interest. What is the interest rate?

26. Suppose you invested some money at 8% simple interest for five years. If you received $500 in interest, how much money did you invest?

Write an equation to model each question and solve.

27. What is 7% of 480? **28.** What percent of 80 is 48? **29.** 90% of what is 27?

30. What is 150% of 26? **31.** 125% of what is 175? **32.** What is 10.25% of 280?

33. What is 35% of 360? **34.** What percent of 36 is 9? **35.** 75% of what is 90?

36. 45% of what is 36? **37.** What is 80% of 120? **38.** What percent of 20 is 8?

39. 25% of what is 92? **40.** What percent of 30 is 90? **41.** What is 39% of 800?

Practice 4-4

Find each percent of change. Describe the percent of change as an increase or decrease. Round to the nearest whole number.

1. 36 g to 27 g

2. 40 cm to 100 cm

3. 90 in. to 45 in.

4. 500 lb to 1500 lb

5. $90 to $84.50

6. $100 to $140

7. $15 to $5.50

8. 100 mi to 175 mi

9. 280 m to 320 m

10. 58 to 76

11. 60 to 150

12. 600 mi to 480 mi

13. 18 to 27

14. 290 yd to 261 yd

15. 26.2 to 22.8

16. $8.50 to $12.75

17. $36\frac{1}{2}$ to $29\frac{1}{4}$

18. $74\frac{3}{4}$ to $66\frac{1}{2}$

19. $6\frac{3}{4}$ to $8\frac{1}{4}$

20. $15\frac{1}{2}$ to $18\frac{1}{4}$

Find each percent of change. Describe the percent of change as an increase or decrease. Round to the nearest whole number.

21. In 1985, the average price for gasoline was $1.20/gal. In 2000, the average price for gasoline was $1.56. Find the percent of change.

22. In 1980, Texas had 27 U.S. Representatives. That number increased to 30 in 2000. Find the percent of change.

23. In 1980, the average annual tuition charge for a four-year public university was $840. The average annual tuition charge in 2000 was $3356. What is the percent of change?

24. The United States imported 6,909,000 barrels of oil per day in 1980. In 2000, the United States imported 11,459,000 barrels of oil per day. What is the percent of change?

25. In 1977, the average number of households with cable television was 16.6%. In 2000, the average number of households with cable television was 68%. What is the percent of change?

26. In 1989, there were 38,000 licensed drivers under the age of 16. In 1999, the total number of licensed drivers under 16 was 33,248. Find the percent of change.

27. In 1990, Atlanta, GA, failed to meet air quality standards on 42 days. In 1999, Atlanta failed to meet air quality standards on 61 days. What is the percent of change?

Find the greatest possible error and the percent error for each measurement.

28. 3 cm

29. 0.5 cm

30. 6 cm

31. 16 in.

32. 36.85 g

33. 0.9 cm

Find the minimum and maximum possible areas for rectangles with the following measurements.

34. 8 cm × 10 cm

35. 3 in. × 5 in.

36. 8 m × 12 m

Find the minimum and maximum possible volume for a rectangular solid with the following measurements.

37. 16 in. × 22 in. × 18 in.

38. 13 cm × 15 cm × 18 cm

39. 3 m × 4 m × 5 m

Algebra 1 Chapter 4

Practice 4-5

A driver collected data on how long it takes to drive to work.

Time in minutes	20	25	30
Number of trips	4	8	2

1. Find P(the trip will take 25 min).

2. Find P(the trip will take 20 min).

3. Find P(the trip will take at least 25 min).

Use the data in the line plot to find each probability.

Student Birth Months

					X					X
X		X			X			X		X
X		X			X	X		X	X	X
X	X	X	X		X	X	X	X	X	X
JAN	FEB	MAR	APR	MAY	JUN	JUL	AUG	SEP	OCT	NOV	DEC

4. P(June)

5. P(October)

6. P(first six months of year)

7. P(May)

8. P(not December)

9. P(last three months of year)

A cereal manufacturer selects 100 boxes of cereal at random. Ninety-nine of the boxes are the correct weight. Find each probability.

10. P(the cereal box is the correct weight)

11. P(the cereal box is not the correct weight)

12. There are 24,000 boxes of cereal. Predict how many of the boxes are the correct weight.

13. One letter is chosen at random from the word *ALGEBRA*. Find each probability.

    a. P(the letter is A)

    b. P(the letter is a vowel)

14. Patrice has a 40% chance of making a free throw. What is the probability that she will miss the free throw?

15. A box of animal crackers contains five hippos, two lions, three zebras, and four elephants. Find the probability if one animal cracker is chosen at random.

    a. P(a hippo)

    b. P(not an elephant)

    c. P(an elephant or a lion)

16. Anthony is making a collage for his art class by picking shapes randomly. He has five squares, two triangles, two ovals, and four circles. Find each probability.

    a. P(circle is chosen first)

    b. P(a square is not chosen first)

    c. P(a triangle or a square is chosen first)

Practice 4-6

Probability of Compound Events

1. Suppose you have a dark closet containing seven blue shirts, five yellow shirts, and eight white shirts. You pick two shirts from the closet. Find each probability.

   a. P(blue then yellow) with replacing
   b. P(blue then yellow) without replacing
   c. P(yellow then yellow) with replacing
   d. P(yellow then yellow) without replacing
   e. P(yellow then white) with replacing
   f. P(yellow then white) without replacing
   g. P(blue then blue) with replacing
   h. P(blue then blue) without replacing

A and B are independent events. Find the missing probability.

2. $P(A) = \frac{3}{7}, P(A \text{ and } B) = \frac{1}{3}$. Find $P(B)$.

3. $P(B) = \frac{1}{5}, P(A \text{ and } B) = \frac{2}{13}$. Find $P(A)$.

4. $P(B) = \frac{15}{16}, P(A \text{ and } B) = \frac{3}{4}$. Find $P(A)$.

5. $P(A) = \frac{8}{15}, P(B) = \frac{3}{4}$. Find $P(A \text{ and } B)$.

6. Suppose you draw two tennis balls from a bag containing seven pink, four white, three yellow, and two striped balls. Find each probability.

   a. P(yellow then pink) with replacing
   b. P(yellow then pink) without replacing
   c. P(pink then pink) with replacing
   d. P(pink then pink) without replacing
   e. P(striped then striped) with replacing
   f. P(striped then striped) without replacing
   g. P(pink then white) with replacing
   h. P(pink then white) without replacing

A and B are independent events. Find the missing probability.

7. $P(A) = \frac{3}{4}, P(A \text{ and } B) = \frac{1}{2}$. Find $P(B)$.

8. $P(A) = \frac{3}{7}, P(B) = \frac{1}{6}$. Find $P(A \text{ and } B)$.

9. $P(B) = \frac{9}{10}, P(A \text{ and } B) = \frac{3}{5}$. Find $P(A)$.

10. $P(B) = \frac{1}{4}, P(A \text{ and } B) = \frac{3}{20}$. Find $P(A)$.

Use an equation to solve each problem.

11. A bag contains green and yellow color tiles. You pick two tiles without replacing the first one. The probability that the first tile is yellow is $\frac{3}{5}$. The probability of drawing two yellow tiles is $\frac{12}{35}$. Find the probability that the second tile you pick is yellow.

12. A bag contains red and blue marbles. You pick two marbles without replacing the first one. The probability of drawing a blue and then a red is $\frac{4}{15}$. The probability that your second marble is red if your first marble is blue is $\frac{2}{3}$. Find the probability that the first marble is blue.

Practice 5-1

The graph shows the speed a student traveled on the way to school.

1. What do the flat parts of the graph represent?

2. Circle the sections of the graph that show the speed decreasing.

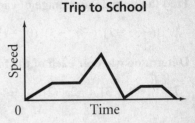
Trip to School

The graph shows the relationship between time and distance from home.

3. What do the flat parts of the graph represent?

4. What do the sections from 3 P.M. to 4 P.M. and from 5 P.M. to 6 P.M. represent?

5. What does the section from 12 P.M. to 1 P.M. represent?

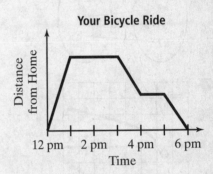
Your Bicycle Ride

Sketch a graph to describe the following. Explain the activity in each section of the graph.

6. your elevation above sea level as you hike in the mountains

7. your speed as you travel from home to school

8. the height of an airplane above the ground flying from Dallas, Texas to Atlanta, Georgia

9. the speed of a person driving to the store and having to stop at two stoplights

The graph shows the relationship between time and speed for an airplane.

10. Circle the sections of the graph that show the speed increasing.

11. Circle the section of the graph that shows the plane not moving.

12. Circle the section of the graph that shows the plane moving at a constant speed.

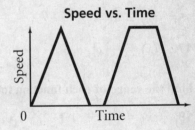
Speed vs. Time

Practice 5-2

Find the domain and range of each relation.

1. $\{(-3, -7), (-1, -3), (0, -1), (2, 3), (4, 7)\}$

2. $\{(-5, -4), (-4, 2), (0, 2), (1, 3), (2, 4)\}$

Determine whether each of the following relations is a function.

3. $\left\{ (-4, -3), (-2, -2), (0, -1), \left(1, -\frac{1}{2}\right) \right\}$

4. $\{(0, 0), (1, 1), (4, 2), (1, -1)\}$

5.
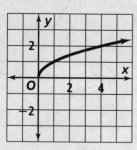

6.
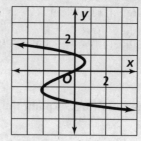

7.
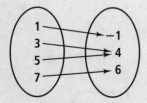

8.

Evaluate each function rule for $x = 3$.

9. $f(x) = 2x - 15$

10. $f(x) = -x + 3$

11. $g(x) = \frac{2}{3}x - 1$

12. $h(x) = -\frac{1}{2}x - \frac{1}{2}$

13. $h(x) = -0.1x + 2.1$

14. $g(x) = -\frac{x}{6} + \frac{3}{2}$

Evaluate each function rule for $x = -\frac{1}{2}$.

15. $f(x) = 4x - 2$

16. $f(x) = -\frac{1}{2}x + 1$

17. $g(x) = -|x| + 3$

18. $h(x) = x - \frac{1}{2}$

Find the range of each function for the given domain.

19. $f(x) = -3x + 1; \{-2, -1, 0\}$

20. $f(x) = x^2 + x - 2; \{-2, 0, 1\}$

21. $h(x) = -x^2; \{-3, -1, 1\}$

22. $g(x) = -\frac{1}{2}|x| + 1; \{-2, -1, 1\}$

23. For a car traveling at a constant rate of 60 mi/h, the distance traveled is a function of the time traveled.

 a. Express this relation as a function.

 b. Find the range of the function when the domain is $\{1, 5, 10\}$.

 c. What do the domain and range represent?

Practice 5-3

Function Rules, Tables, and Graphs

Model each rule with a table of values and a graph.

1. $f(x) = x + 1$ **2.** $f(x) = 2x$ **3.** $f(x) = 3x - 2$

4. $f(x) = \frac{3}{2}x - 2$ **5.** $f(x) = \frac{1}{2}x$ **6.** $f(x) = -\frac{2}{3}x + 1$

7. $f(x) = x^2 + 1$ **8.** $f(x) = -x^2 + 2$ **9.** $f(x) = x - 3$

10. Suppose a van gets 22 mi/gal. The distance traveled $D(g)$ is a function of the gallons of gas used.

    a. Use the rule $D(g) = 22g$ to make a table of values and then a graph.

    b. How far did the van travel if it used 10.5 gallons of gas?

    c. Should the points of the graph be connected by a line? Explain.

11. The admission to a fairgrounds is $3.00 per vehicle plus $.50 per passenger. The total admission is a function of the number of passengers.

    a. Use the rule $T(n) = 3 + 0.50n$ to make a table of values and then a graph.

    b. What is the admission for a car with six people in it?

    c. Should the points of the graph be connected by a line? Explain.

Graph each function.

12. $f(x) = 4x + 2$ **13.** $f(x) = |-2x|$ **14.** $f(x) = -3x + 7$

15. $f(x) = -|x| - 1$ **16.** $f(x) = 8 - \frac{3}{4}x$ **17.** $f(x) = \frac{2}{3}x - 7$

18. $f(x) = -\frac{2}{3}x + 6$ **19.** $f(x) = x^2 - 2x + 1$ **20.** $f(x) = -\frac{1}{2}x + 3$

21. $y = -x^2 + 1$ **22.** $y = 9 - x^2$ **23.** $y = 2x^2 + x - 2$

Make a table of values for each graph.

24.
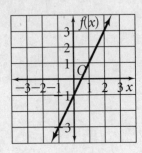

25.
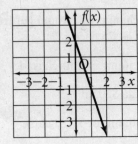

26.
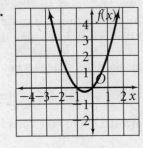

Practice 5-4

Writing a Function Rule

Write a function rule for each table.

1.

x	f(x)
0	3
2	5
4	7
6	9

2.

x	f(x)
0	0
1	3
3	9
5	15

3.

x	f(x)
5	0
10	5
15	10
20	15

4. a. Write a function rule to calculate the cost of buying bananas at $.39 a pound.

b. How much would it cost to buy 3.5 pounds of bananas?

5. To rent a cabin, a resort charges $50 plus $10 per person.

a. Write a function rule to calculate the total cost of renting the cabin.

b. Use your rule to find the total cost for six people to stay in the cabin.

Write a function rule for each table.

6.

x	f(x)
−4	−2
−2	−1
6	3
8	4

7.

x	f(x)
−3	9
0	0
1	1
5	25

8.

x	f(x)
0	20
2	18
4	16
8	12

9. Pens are shipped to the office supply store in boxes of 12 each.

a. Write a function rule to calculate the total number of pens when you know the number of boxes.

b. Calculate the total number of pens in 16 boxes.

10. a. Write a function rule to determine the change you would get from a $20 bill when purchasing items that cost $1.25 each.

b. Calculate the change when five of these items are purchased.

c. Can you purchase 17 of these items with a $20 bill?

11. You invest $209 to buy shirts and then sell them for $9.50 each.

a. Write a function rule to determine your profit.

b. Use your rule to find your profit after selling 24 shirts.

c. How many shirts do you need to sell to get back your investment?

Practice 5-5

Direct Variation

• •

Is each equation a direct variation? If it is, find the constant of variation.

1. $y = 5x$

2. $8x + 2y = 0$

3. $y = \frac{3}{4}x - 7$

4. $y = 2x + 5$

5. $3x - y = 0$

6. $y = \frac{3}{5}x$

7. $-3x + 2y = 0$

8. $-5x + 2y = 9$

9. $8x + 4y = 12$

10. $6x - 3y = 0$

11. $x - 3y = 6$

12. $9x + 5y = 0$

The ordered pairs in each exercise are for the same direct variation. Find each missing value.

13. $(3, 2)$ and $(6, y)$

14. $(-2, 8)$ and $(x, 12)$

15. $(4, y)$ and $(16, 12)$

16. $(x, 8)$ and $(6, -16)$

17. $(3, y)$ and $(9, 15)$

18. $(2, y)$ and $(10, 15)$

19. $(-4, 3)$ and $(x, 6)$

20. $(3, y)$ and $(1.5, 6)$

21. $\left(\frac{2}{3}, 2\right)$ and $(x, 6)$

22. $(2.5, 5)$ and $(x, 9)$

23. $(4.8, 5)$ and $(2.4, y)$

24. $(9, 3)$ and $(x, -2)$

For the data in each table, tell whether y varies directly with x. If it does, write an equation for the direct variation.

25.

x	y
4	8
7	14
10	20

26.

x	y
−3	−2
3	2
9	6

27.

x	y
4	3
5	4.5
11	13.5

28.

x	y
−2	−2.8
3	4.2
8	11.2

29. Charles's Law states that at constant pressure, the volume of a fixed amount of gas varies directly with its temperature measured in degrees Kelvin. A gas has a volume of 250 mL at 300° K.

    a. Write an equation for the relationship between volume and temperature.

    b. What is the volume if the temperature increases to 420° K?

30. Your percent grade varies directly with the number of correct answers. You got a grade of 80 when you had 20 correct answers.

    a. Write an equation for the relationship between percent grade and number of correct answers.

    b. What would your percent grade be with 24 correct answers?

31. The amount of simple interest earned in a savings account varies directly with the amount of money in the savings account. You have $1000 in your savings account and earn $50 in simple interest. How much interest would you earn if you had $1500 in your savings account?

Practice 5-6

Find the common difference of each arithmetic sequence.

1. $10, 16, 22, 28, \ldots$

2. $9, 6, 3, 0, \ldots$

3. $-12, -17, -22, -27, \ldots$

4. $-11, -8, -5, -2, \ldots$

5. $4, 4\frac{1}{2}, 5, 5\frac{1}{2}, \ldots$

6. $7\frac{1}{2}, 7, 6\frac{1}{2}, 6, \ldots$

7. $9, 10.5, 12, 13.5, \ldots$

8. $1, -1.5, -4, -6.5, \ldots$

9. $8, 9.1, 10.2, 11.3, \ldots$

10. $-9, -8.1, -7.2, -6.3, \ldots$

11. $-3, -0.6, 1.8, 4.2, \ldots$

12. $6.2, 4.5, 2.8, 1.1, \ldots$

Find the next two terms in each sequence.

13. $1, 7, 13, 19, \ldots$

14. $-8, -5, -2, 1, \ldots$

15. $1, -4, -9, -14, \ldots$

16. $\frac{1}{2}, -\frac{1}{2}, -\frac{3}{2}, -\frac{5}{2}, \ldots$

17. $2.7, 4, 5.3, 6.6, \ldots$

18. $9.8, 0.7, -8.4, -17.5, \ldots$

19. $6\frac{1}{3}, 4\frac{2}{3}, 3, 1\frac{1}{3}, \ldots$

20. $2\frac{1}{2}, \frac{3}{4}, -1, -2\frac{3}{4}, \ldots$

Find the fifth, tenth, and hundredth terms of each sequence.

21. $4, 14, 24, 34, \ldots$

22. $14, 6, -2, -10, \ldots$

23. $3, 10, 17, 24, \ldots$

24. $-19, -22, -25, -28, \ldots$

25. $\frac{1}{4}, -\frac{1}{4}, -\frac{3}{4}, -\frac{5}{4}, \ldots$

26. $-1.3, -0.3, 0.7, 1.7, \ldots$

27. $0, 101, 202, 303, \ldots$

28. $-1, -100, -199, -298, \ldots$

29. $5, 3.9, 2.8, 1.7, \ldots$

30. $-3\frac{1}{2}, -3\frac{3}{4}, -4, -4\frac{1}{4}, \ldots$

Determine whether each sequence is arithmetic. Justify your answer.

31. $0.5, 0.3, 0.1, -0.1, \ldots$

32. $-1, 1, -1, 1, \ldots$

33. $3, 6, 12, 24, \ldots$

34. $100, 81, 64, 49, \ldots$

35. Renting a backhoe costs a flat fee of $65 plus an additional $35 per hour.

    a. Write the first four terms of a sequence that represents the total cost of renting the backhoe for 1, 2, 3, and 4 hours.

    b. What is the common difference?

    c. What are the 5th, 24th, 48th, and 72nd terms in the sequence?

Practice 6-1

Find the slope of each line.

1.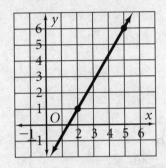

2.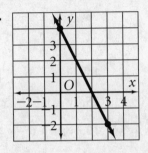

3.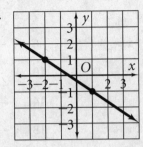

4.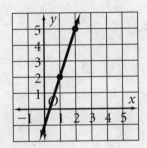

5.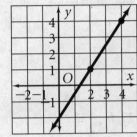

6.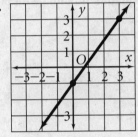

Find the slope of the line that passes through each pair of points.

7. $(1, 2), (4, 3)$

8. $(7, 2), (3, 5)$

9. $(0, 2), (4, 6)$

10. $(-2, 5), (3, -4)$

11. $(2, 4), (6, 7)$

12. $(-2, -5), (4, 5)$

13. $(-3, -2), (4, -2)$

14. $(4, -2), (4, 9)$

15. $(5, 2), (8, -4)$

Find the rate of change. Explain what the rate of change means for each situation.

16.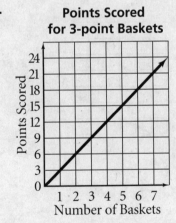

17.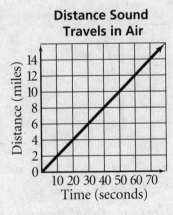

18.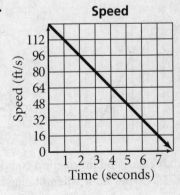

Find the slope of the line that passes through each pair of points.

19. $(0, 0), (3, 7)$

20. $(-2, 4), (4, -1)$

21. $(-3, 6), (1, -2)$

22. $(2, 4), (4, -4)$

23. $(2, -10), (5, -6)$

24. $(5, 1), (11, 1)$

25. $(3, 7), (3, 5)$

26. $(7, 9), (2, 9)$

27. $(-5, -2), (-5, 3)$

Name _____ Class _____ Date _____

Practice 6-2

Slope-Intercept Form

Find the slope and *y*-intercept of each equation. Then graph.

1. $y = x + 2$ **2.** $y + 3 = -\frac{1}{3}x$ **3.** $y = 2x - 1$ **4.** $y - \frac{3}{5}x = -1$

5. $y = \frac{1}{2}x - 4$ **6.** $y - 2x = -3$ **7.** $y = \frac{2}{5}x + 3$ **8.** $y + \frac{1}{3}x = -2$

9. $y = -x - 2$ **10.** $y - 6 = -2x$ **11.** $y = -5x - 2$ **12.** $y + x = 0$

13. $y + 4 = 2x$ **14.** $y = -5x + 5$ **15.** $y = -4 + x$ **16.** $y = -4x$

17. $y = \frac{4}{5}x + 2$ **18.** $y - \frac{3}{4}x = -5$ **19.** $y = -6$ **20.** $y - 3 = -\frac{2}{3}x$

21. $y = -\frac{7}{4}x + 6$ **22.** $y + 3x = 6$ **23.** $y + \frac{1}{5}x = -2$ **24.** $y = \frac{3}{7}x$

Write an equation of a line with the given slope and *y*-intercept.

25. $m = 4, b = 8$ **26.** $m = -2, b = -6$ **27.** $m = \frac{4}{3}, b = 0$

28. $m = -\frac{9}{5}, b = -7$ **29.** $m = -6, b = 1$ **30.** $m = \frac{3}{7}, b = -1$

31. $m = -\frac{1}{5}, b = -3$ **32.** $m = 9, b = 4$ **33.** $m = -8, b = 11$

34. $m = \frac{2}{9}, b = 0$ **35.** $m = -11, b = 13$ **36.** $m = -\frac{7}{2}, b = -6$

Write the slope-intercept form of the equation for each line.

37. 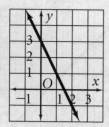   **38.** 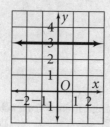   **39.**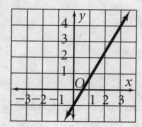

40. 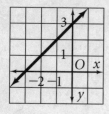   **41.** 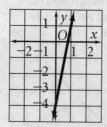   **42.**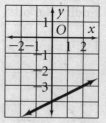

43. A television production company charges a basic fee of $4000 and then $2000 per hour when filming a commercial.

  a. Write an equation in slope-intercept form relating the basic fee and per-hour charge.

  b. Graph your equation.

  c. Use your graph to find the production costs if 4 hours of filming were needed.

Practice 6-3

Graph each equation using *x*- and *y*-intercepts.

1. $x + y = 3$ **2.** $x + 3y = -3$ **3.** $-2x + 3y = 6$ **4.** $5x - 4y = -20$

5. $3x + 4y = 12$ **6.** $7x + 3y = 21$ **7.** $y = -2.5$ **8.** $2x - 3y = 4$

9. $x = 3$ **10.** $3x - 2y = -6$ **11.** $5x + 2y = 5$ **12.** $-7x + 2y = 14$

13. $3x + y = 3$ **14.** $-3x + 5y = 15$ **15.** $2x + y = 3$ **16.** $8x - 3y = 24$

17. $3x - 5y = 15$ **18.** $x + 4y = 4$ **19.** $x = -3.5$ **20.** $y = 6$

Write each equation in standard form using integers.

21. $y = 4x - 11$ **22.** $y = 2x - 6$ **23.** $y = -2x - 3$ **24.** $y = 5x - 32$

25. $y = \frac{2}{3}x - \frac{25}{3}$ **26.** $y = 43 - 4x$ **27.** $y = -\frac{4}{5}x + \frac{6}{5}$ **28.** $y = -\frac{x}{5}$

29. $y = \frac{5}{2}x - 22$ **30.** $y = \frac{7}{3}x + \frac{25}{3}$ **31.** $y = -\frac{x}{3} + \frac{2}{3}$ **32.** $y = -6x - 38$

33. The drama club sells 200 lb of fruit to raise money. The fruit is sold in 5-lb bags and 10-lb bags.

    a. Write an equation to find the number of each type of bag that the club should sell.

    b. Graph your equation.

    c. Use your graph to find two different combinations of types of bags.

34. The student council is sponsoring a carnival to raise money. Tickets cost $5 for adults and $3 for students. The student council wants to raise $450.

    a. Write an equation to find the number of each type of ticket they should sell.

    b. Graph your equation.

    c. Use your graph to find two different combinations of tickets sold.

35. Anna goes to a store to buy $70 worth of flour and sugar for her bakery. A bag of flour costs $5, and a bag of sugar costs $7.

    a. Write an equation to find the number of bags of each type Anna can buy.

    b. Graph your equation.

36. You have $50 to spend on cold cuts for a party. Ham costs $5.99/lb, and turkey costs $4.99/lb. Write an equation in standard form to relate the number of pounds of each kind of meat you could buy.

Practice 6-4

Point-Slope Form and Writing Linear Equations

Write an equation in point-slope form for the line through the given points or through the given point with the given slope.

1. $(5, 7), (6, 8)$ **2.** $(-2, 3); m = -1$ **3.** $(1, 2), (3, 8)$ **4.** $(-2, 3); m = 4$

5. $(4, 7); m = \frac{3}{2}$ **6.** $(6, -2); m = -\frac{4}{3}$ **7.** $(0, 5), (-3, 2)$ **8.** $(8, 11), (6, 16)$

9. $(4, 2), (-4, -2)$ **10.** $(15, 16), (13, 10)$ **11.** $(0, -7); m = -4$ **12.** $(-3, 4), (1, 6)$

13. $(1, 2); m$ undefined   **14.** $(-6, 7); m = -\frac{1}{2}$ **15.** $(21, -2), (27, 2)$ **16.** $(7, 5); m = 0$

17. $(8, -2), (14, 1)$ **18.** $(4, 8), (2, 12)$ **19.** $(-5, 13), (-10, 9)$ **20.** $(6, 2); m = \frac{3}{4}$

21. $(5, -3); m = -2$ **22.** $(4, 3.5); m = 0.5$ **23.** $(-6, 2); m = \frac{5}{3}$ **24.** $(100, 90), (80, 120)$

25. $(-3, 6), (3, -6)$ **26.** $(11, 7), (9, 3)$ **27.** $(2, 7); m = \frac{5}{2}$ **28.** $(-9, 8); m = -\frac{5}{3}$

Is the relationship shown by the data linear? If it is, model the data with an equation.

29.

x	y
2	3
3	7
4	11
5	15

30.

x	y
−3	4
−1	6
1	7
3	10

31.

x	y
−4	12
−1	8
5	−4
10	−8

32.

x	y
−2	5
3	−5
7	−13
11	−21

33.

x	y
−6	−5
−2	1
0	4
8	16

34.

x	y
−6	11
−3	9
6	3
15	−3

35.

x	y
−7	−3
−5	0
−1	3
3	7

36.

x	y
−4	1
2	4
6	6
14	10

Write an equation of each line in point-slope form.

37.

38.

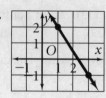

39.

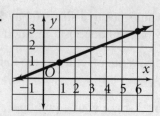

Name _____ Class _____ Date _____

Practice 6-5

• •

Find the slope of a line parallel to the graph of each equation.

1. $y = 4x + 2$
2. $y = \frac{2}{7}x + 1$
3. $y = -9x - 13$
4. $y = -\frac{1}{2}x + 1$

5. $6x + 2y = 4$
6. $y - 3 = 0$
7. $-5x + 5y = 4$
8. $9x - 5y = 4$

9. $-x + 3y = 6$
10. $6x - 7y = 10$
11. $x = -4$
12. $-3x - 5y = 6$

Write an equation for the line that is perpendicular to the given line and that passes through the given point.

13. $(6, 4); y = 3x - 2$
14. $(-5, 5); y = -5x + 9$
15. $(-1, -4); y = \frac{1}{6}x + 1$

16. $(1, 1); y = -\frac{1}{4}x + 7$
17. $(12, -6); y = 4x + 1$
18. $(0, -3); y = -\frac{4}{3}x - 7$

19.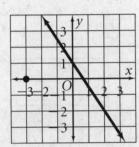
20.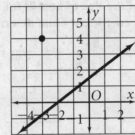
21.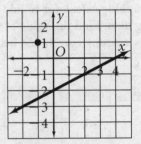

Write an equation for the line that is parallel to the given line and that passes through the given point.

22. $(3, 4); y = 2x - 7$
23. $(1, 3); y = -4x + 5$
24. $(4, -1); y = x - 3$

25. $(4, 0); y = \frac{3}{2}x + 9$
26. $(-8, -4); y = -\frac{3}{4}x + 5$
27. $(9, -7); -7x - 3y = 3$

28.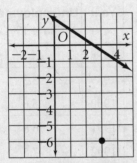
29.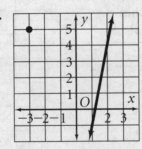
30.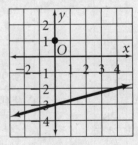

Tell whether the lines for each pair of equations are *parallel*, *perpendicular*, or *neither*.

31. $y = 3x - 8$
$3x - y = -1$

32. $3x + 2y = -5$
$y = \frac{2}{3}x + 6$

33. $y = -\frac{5}{2}x + 11$
$-5x + 2y = 20$

34. $9x + 3y = 6$
$3x + 9y = 6$

35. $y = -4$
$y = 4$

36. $x = 10$
$y = -2$

• •

Practice 6-6

Scatter Plots and Equations of Lines

Decide whether the data in each scatter plot follow a linear pattern. If they do, find the equation of a trend line.

1.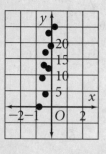

2.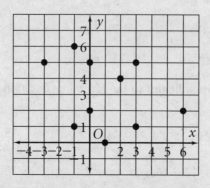

3.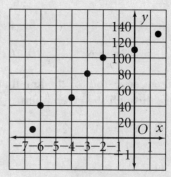

Use a graphing calculator to find the equation of the line of best fit for the following data. Find the value of the correlation coefficient r and determine if there is a strong correlation between the data.

4.

x	y
1	7
2	5
3	−1
4	3
5	−5

5.

x	y
1	6
2	15
3	−5
4	1
5	−2

6.

x	y
1	5
4	8
8	3
13	10
19	13

7.

x	y
12	28
15	50
18	14
21	28
24	36

Draw a scatter plot. Write the equation of the trend line.

8.

x	y
1	17
2	20
3	22
4	26
5	28
6	31

9.

Year	U.S. Union Membership (millions)
1988	17.00
1989	16.96
1990	16.74
1991	16.57
1992	16.39
1993	16.60
1994	16.75
1995	16.36
1996	16.27
1997	16.11
1998	16.21

Source: *World Almanac 2000*, p. 154.

10.

x	y
1	18
2	20
3	24
4	30
5	28
6	33

11.

Year	U.S. Unemployment Rate (%)
1988	5.5
1989	5.3
1990	5.6
1991	6.8
1992	7.5
1993	6.9
1994	6.1
1995	5.6
1996	5.4
1997	4.9
1998	4.5

Source: *World Almanac 2000*, p. 145.

Practice 6-7

Graph each equation by translating $y = |x|$.

1. $y = |x| - 3$ **2.** $y = |x| + 4$ **3.** $y = |x| - 1$

4. $y = |x| + \frac{1}{2}$ **5.** $y = |x| + 2\frac{1}{2}$ **6.** $y = |x| + 3$

7. $y = |x + 2|$ **8.** $y = |x - 4|$ **9.** $y = |3x|$

10. $y = |x + 3| - 2$ **11.** $y = |x - 2| + 1$ **12.** $y = |x - 3| + 2$

Graph each equation by translating $y = -|x|$.

13. $y = -|x| + 1$ **14.** $y = -|x + 2|$ **15.** $y = -|x| - 5$

16. $y = -|x - 4| + 2$ **17.** $y = -|x - 5|$ **18.** $y = -|x| + 4.5$

19. $y = -|x - 3| + 1$ **20.** $y = -|x + 1| + 3$ **21.** $y = -|x + 2| - 4$

Write an equation for each translation of $y = |x|$.

22. left 7 units   **23.** right 5 units   **24.** up 6 units

25. up 2 units, right 3 units   **26.** down 3 units, left 1 unit   **27.** down 1 unit, right 2 units

28. left 2 units, up 4 units   **29.** right 3 units, up 2 units   **30.** left 4 units, down 3.5 units

Write an equation for each translation of $y = -|x|$.

31. 3 units up   **32.** 3.5 units left   **33.** $\frac{3}{4}$ unit down

34. down 3 units   **35.** up 2 units, right 1 unit   **36.** down 5 units, left 1 unit

37. right 3 units, up 2 units   **38.** down 4 units, left 2 units   **39.** up 4 units, right 3 units

Write an equation for the given graphs.

40.
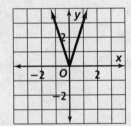

41.
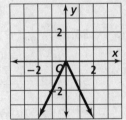

42.
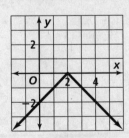

43.
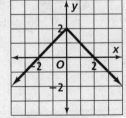

Practice 7-1

Solve by graphing. Write *no solution* or *infinitely many solutions* where appropriate.

1. $y = 3x - 1$
$y = -2x + 4$

2. $y = x - 1$
$y = -x + 7$

3. $y = \frac{3}{4}x + 2$
$\frac{3}{4}x - y = 4$

4. $y = 4x + 7$
$y = -3x$

5. $y = x - 3$
$y = \frac{1}{7}x + 3$

6. $y = -3x - 4$
$3x + y = -4$

7. $y = -x - 3$
$y = -2x - 8$

8. $y = -x + 2$
$3x + 3y = 12$

9. $y = x$
$y = 3x + 2$

10. $y = 4x - 3$
$y = -3x - 3$

11. $y = \frac{5}{3}x - 4$
$y = 2x - 6$

12. $y = 3x + 2$
$2x + y = -8$

13. $x = y + 4$
$y = x + 4$

14. $x + y = 2$
$y = -2x - 1$

15. $2x - y = 3$
$y = x + 4$

16. $3x - 6y = 12$
$2x - 4y = 8$

17. $x - y = 1$
$y = \frac{3}{4}x + 1$

18. $y = x$
$x = 2y + 2$

19. $3x - y = 9$
$y = x + 1$

20. $2x + y = 0$
$y = 2x - 4$

21. $y = 2x - 6$
$x + y = 9$

22. $y = -x$
$y = 3x + 12$

23. $4x + y = 6$
$y = -4x - 1$

24. $y = 4x$
$y = -3x$

25. $y = x$
$2x + y = \frac{3}{2}$

26. $3x + y = 6$
$2x - y = \frac{3}{2}$

27. $x + 4y = -\frac{1}{2}$
$-2x - 3y = 1$

28. $x - y = -\frac{3}{2}$
$-2x + 5y = -4.5$

Solve each system by using a graphing calculator. Write *no solution* or *infinitely many solutions* where appropriate.

29. $y = x + 6$
$y = 2x - 7$

30. $y = \frac{7}{2}x - 6$
$y = 3x - 2$

31. $y = 2x - 20$
$y = -x + 34$

32. $y = \frac{2}{3}x + 4$
$2x - 3y = 3$

33. $y = -x - 5$
$y = 3x - 105$

34. $x + y = -10$
$2x + 3y = -30$

35. $3x - 4y = 0$
$2x + y = 110$

36. $y = \frac{1}{7}x + 10$
$x - 2y = 0$

37. $2x + y = 6$
$3y = -6x + 9$

38. $y = \frac{5}{6}x + 12$
$y = \frac{4}{3}x - 6$

39. $2x - y = 8$
$3x - 2y = 0$

40. $x + 2y = 2$
$3x + 4y = 22$

41. $y = 2x + 0.75$
$y = -4x - 8.25$

42. $1.25x + 3.25y = -5.75$
$0.5x - 1.5y = 0.5$

43. $x = -2y - 3.5$
$-5x + 3y = -15$

Practice 7-2

Solving Systems Using Substitution

Solve each system using substitution. Write *no solution* or *infinitely many solutions* where appropriate.

1. $y = x$
$y = -x + 2$

2. $y = x + 4$
$y = 3x$

3. $y = 3x - 10$
$y = 2x - 5$

4. $x = -2y + 1$
$x = y - 5$

5. $y = 5x + 5$
$y = 15x - 1$

6. $y = x - 3$
$y = -3x + 25$

7. $y = x - 7$
$2x + y = 8$

8. $y = 3x - 6$
$-3x + y = -6$

9. $x + 2y = 200$
$x = y + 50$

10. $3x + y = 10$
$y = -3x + 4$

11. $y = 2x + 7$
$y = 5x + 4$

12. $3x - 2y = 0$
$x + y = -5$

13. $4x + 2y = 8$
$y = -2x + 4$

14. $6x - 3y = 6$
$y = 2x + 5$

15. $2x + 4y = -6$
$x - 3y = 7$

16. $5x - 3y = -4$
$x + y = -4$

17. $y = -\frac{2}{3}x + 4$
$2x + 3y = -6$

18. $2x + 3y = 8$
$\frac{3}{2}y = 4 - x$

19. $3x - y = 4$
$2x + y = 16$

20. $x + y = 0$
$x = y + 4$

21. $5x + 2y = 6$
$y = -\frac{5}{2}x + 1$

22. $2x + 5y = -6$
$4x + y = -12$

23. $4x + 3y = -3$
$2x + y = -1$

24. $y = -\frac{2}{3}x + 1$
$4x + 6y = 6$

25. $5x - 6y = 19$
$4x + 3y = 10$

26. $2x + y = 6.6$
$5x - 2y = 0.3$

27. $2x - 4y = 3.8$
$3x - y = 17.7$

28. $3x + 4y = 8$
$4.5x + 6y = 12$

29. $3x - 4y = -5$
$x = y + 2$

30. $y = \frac{1}{3}x + 10$
$x = 3y + 6$

31. $2x + 5y = 62$
$3x - y = 23.3$

32. $-5x + y = 6$
$2x - 3y = 60$

33. $x = \frac{3}{4}y - 6$
$y = \frac{4}{3}x + 8$

34. $5x + 6y = -76$
$x + 2y = -44$

35. $3x - 2y = 10$
$y = \frac{3}{2}x - 1$

36. $-3x + 2y = -6$
$-2x + y = 6$

37. At an ice cream parlor, ice cream cones cost $1.10 and sundaes cost $2.35. One day, the receipts for a total of 172 cones and sundaes were $294.20. How many cones were sold?

38. You purchase 8 gal of paint and 3 brushes for $152.50. The next day, you purchase 6 gal of paint and 2 brushes for $113.00. How much does each gallon of paint and each brush cost?

Practice 7-3

Solving Systems Using Elimination

Solve by elimination. Show your work.

1. $x + 2y = 7$
$3x - 2y = -3$

2. $3x + y = 20$
$x + y = 12$

3. $5x + 7y = 77$
$5x + 3y = 53$

4. $2x + 5y = -1$
$x + 2y = 0$

5. $3x + 6y = 6$
$2x - 3y = 4$

6. $2x + y = 3$
$-2x + y = 1$

7. $9x - 3y = 24$
$7x - 3y = 20$

8. $2x + 7y = 5$
$2x + 3y = 9$

9. $x + y = 30$
$x - y = 6$

10. $4x - y = 6$
$3x + 2y = 21$

11. $x + 2y = 9$
$3x + 2y = 7$

12. $3x + 5y = 10$
$x - 5y = -10$

13. $2x - 3y = -11$
$3x + 2y = 29$

14. $8x - 9y = 19$
$4x + y = -7$

15. $2x + 6y = 0$
$-2x - 5y = 0$

16. $-2x + 3y = -9$
$x + 3y = 3$

17. $4x - 3y = 11$
$3x - 5y = -11$

18. $3x + 7y = 48$
$5x - 7y = -32$

19. $-2x + 3y = 25$
$-2x + 6y = 58$

20. $3x + 8y = 81$
$5x - 6y = -39$

21. $8x + 13y = 179$
$2x - 13y = -69$

22. $-x + 8y = -32$
$3x - y = 27$

23. $2x + 7y = -7$
$5x + 7y = 14$

24. $x + 6y = 48$
$-x + y = 8$

25. $6x + 3y = 0$
$-3x + 3y = 9$

26. $7x + 3y = 25$
$-2x - y = -8$

27. $3x - 8y = 32$
$-x + 8y = -16$

28. $4x - 7y = -15$
$-4x - 3y = -15$

29. $5x + 7y = -1$
$4x - 2y = 22$

30. $6x - 3y = 69$
$7x - 3y = 76$

31. $x + 8y = 28$
$-3x + 5y = 3$

32. $8x - 6y = -122$
$-4x + 6y = 94$

33. $2x + 9y = 36$
$2x - y = 16$

34. $-6x + 12y = 120$
$5x - 6y = -48$

35. $-x + 3y = 5$
$-x - 3y = 1$

36. $10x - 4y = 6$
$10x + 3y = 13$

37. $6x + 3y = 27$
$-4x + 7y = 27$

38. $6x - 8y = 40$
$5x + 8y = 48$

39. $3x + y = 27$
$-3x + 4y = -42$

40. $2x + 8y = -42$
$-x + 8y = -63$

41. $5x + 9y = 112$
$3x - 2y = 8$

42. $-3x + 2y = 0$
$-3x + 5y = 9$

43. $8x - 2y = 58$
$6x - 2y = 40$

44. $7x - 9y = -57$
$-7x + 10y = 68$

45. $9x + 3y = 2$
$-9x - y = 0$

46. Shopping at Savers Mart, Lisa buys her children four shirts and three pairs of pants for $85.50. She returns the next day and buys three shirts and five pairs of pants for $115.00. What is the price of each shirt and each pair of pants?

47. Grandma's Bakery sells single-crust apple pies for $6.99 and double-crust cherry pies for $10.99. The total number of pies sold on a busy Friday was 36. If the amount collected for all the pies that day was $331.64, how many of each type were sold?

Practice 7-4

Use a system of linear equations to solve each problem.

1. Your teacher is giving you a test worth 100 points containing 40 questions. There are two-point and four-point questions on the test. How many of each type of question are on the test?

2. Suppose you are starting an office-cleaning service. You have spent $315 on equipment. To clean an office, you use $4 worth of supplies. You charge $25 per office. How many offices must you clean to break even?

3. The math club and the science club had fundraisers to buy supplies for a hospice. The math club spent $135 buying six cases of juice and one case of bottled water. The science club spent $110 buying four cases of juice and two cases of bottled water. How much did a case of juice cost? How much did a case of bottled water cost?

4. On a canoe trip, Rita paddled upstream (against the current) at an average speed of 2 mi/h relative to the riverbank. On the return trip downstream (with the current), her average speed was 3 mi/h. Find Rita's paddling speed in still water and the speed of the river's current.

5. Kay spends 250 min/wk exercising. Her ratio of time spent on aerobics to time spent on weight training is 3 to 2. How many minutes per week does she spend on aerobics? How many minutes per week does she spend on weight training?

6. Suppose you invest $1500 in equipment to put pictures on T-shirts. You buy each T-shirt for $3. After you have placed the picture on a shirt, you sell it for $20. How many T-shirts must you sell to break even?

7. A light plane flew from its home base to an airport 255 miles away. With a head wind, the trip took 1.7 hours. The return trip with a tail wind took 1.5 hours. Find the average airspeed of the plane and the average windspeed.

8. Suppose you bought supplies for a party. Three rolls of streamers and 15 party hats cost $30. Later, you bought 2 rolls of streamers and 4 party hats for $11. How much did each roll of streamers cost? How much did each party hat cost?

9. A new parking lot has spaces for 450 cars. The ratio of spaces for full-sized cars to compact cars is 11 to 4. How many spaces are for full-sized cars? How many spaces are for compact cars?

10. While on vacation, Kevin went for a swim in a nearby lake. Swimming against the current, it took him 8 minutes to swim 200 meters. Swimming back to shore with the current took half as long. Find Kevin's average swimming speed and the speed of the lake's current.

Practice 7-5

Graph each linear inequality.

1. $y \geq -4$

2. $x + y < -2$

3. $y < x$

4. $x > 2$

5. $4x + y > -6$

6. $-3x + y \leq -3$

7. $x + 4y \leq 8$

8. $y > 2x + 6$

9. $y > -x + 2$

10. $2x + 3y < -9$

11. $y \leq \frac{3}{7}x + 2$

12. $4x + 2y < -8$

13. $y \leq \frac{3}{4}x + 1$

14. $x - y > 4$

15. $y \geq -\frac{2}{5}x - 2$

16. Suppose your class is raising money for the Red Cross. You make $5 on each basket of fruit and $3 on each box of cheese that you sell. How many items of each type must you sell to raise more than $150?

   a. Write a linear inequality that describes the situation.

   b. Graph the inequality.

   c. Write two possible solutions to the problem.

17. Suppose you intend to spend no more than $60 buying books. Hardback books cost $12 and paperbacks cost $5. How many books of each type can you buy?

   a. Write a linear inequality that describes the situation.

   b. Graph the inequality.

   c. Write two possible solutions to the problem.

18. Suppose that for your exercise program, you either walk 5 mi/d or ride your bicycle 10 mi/d. How many days will it take you to cover a distance of at least 150 mi?

   a. Write a linear inequality that describes the situation.

   b. Graph the inequality.

   c. Write two possible solutions to the problem.

Graph each linear inequality.

19. $6x - 4y > -16$

20. $y \geq -\frac{1}{4}x - 3$

21. $-5x + 4y < -24$

22. $y < -5x + 6$

23. $6x - 4y < -12$

24. $y \geq -\frac{9}{5}x + 7$

25. $y > \frac{5}{7}x - 3$

26. $y < -5x + 9$

27. $-7x + 3y < -18$

28. $y \geq \frac{6}{5}x - 8$

29. $-12x + 8y < 56$

30. $16x + 6y > 36$

Practice 7-6

Systems of Linear Inequalities

Solve each system by graphing. Show your work.

1. $y < 6$
$y > 3$

2. $x < 7$
$y > 2$

3. $x < 2$
$x > 5$

4. $x + y > -2$
$-x + y < 1$

5. $x + y < 2$
$x + y > 5$

6. $y < -5x + 6$
$y > 2x - 1$

7. $y < 2x - 3$
$-2x + y > 5$

8. $-x + 3y < 12$
$y \geq -x + 4$

9. $y \leq -\frac{1}{2}x + 3$
$y \geq -\frac{5}{3}x + 2$

10. $y \geq \frac{3}{4}x + 1$
$y \geq -\frac{2}{3}x - 1$

11. $6x + 4y > 12$
$-3x + 4y > 12$

12. $3x + y < 6$
$-2x + y < 6$

13. $-4x + 2y < -2$
$-2x + y > 3$

14. $-5x + y > -2$
$4x + y < 1$

15. $y < \frac{9}{5}x - 8$
$-9x + 5y > 25$

16. $5x + 4y < 1$
$8y \geq -10x + 24$

17. $6x + 8y < 32$
$-4x + 6y < 24$

18. $x + 7y < 14$
$x - 6y > -12$

19. In basketball you score 2 points for a field goal and 1 point for a free throw. Suppose that you have scored at least 3 points in every game this season, and have a season high score of 15 points in one game. How many field goals and free throws could you have made in any one game?

   a. Write a system of two inequalities that describes this situation.

   b. Graph the system to show all possible solutions.

   c. Write one possible solution to the problem.

20. Suppose you need to use at least $1.00 worth of stamps to mail a package. You have as many $.03 stamps as you need but only four $.32 stamps. How many of each stamp can you use?

   a. Write a system of two inequalities that describes this situation.

   b. Graph the system to show all possible solutions.

   c. Write one possible solution to the problem.

21. A grandmother wants to spend at least $40 but no more than $60 on school clothes for her grandson. T-shirts sell for $10 and pants sell for $20. How many T-shirts and pants could she buy?

   a. Write a system of two inequalities that describes this situation.

   b. Graph the system to show all possible solutions.

   c. Write two possible solutions to the problem.

Practice 8-1

Zero and Negative Exponents

Simplify each expression.

1. 16^0

2. 4^{-2}

3. 3^{-3}

4. 8^{-4}

5. $\dfrac{1}{2^{-5}}$

6. $\dfrac{4}{4^{-3}}$

7. $\dfrac{3}{6^{-1}}$

8. $\dfrac{2^{-1}}{2^{-5}}$

9. $3 \cdot 8^0$

10. $16 \cdot 2^{-2}$

11. 12^{-1}

12. -7^{-2}

13. $16 \cdot 4^0$

14. 9^0

15. $\dfrac{32^{-1}}{8^{-1}}$

16. $\dfrac{9}{2^{-1}}$

17. $\dfrac{8^{-2}}{4^0}$

18. $\dfrac{9^{-1}}{3^{-2}}$

19. $5(-6)^0$

20. $(3.7)^0$

21. $(-9)^{-2}$

22. $(-4.9)^0$

23. $-6 \cdot 3^{-4}$

24. $\dfrac{7^{-2}}{4^{-1}}$

Evaluate each expression for $a = -2$ and $b = 6$.

25. b^{-2}

26. a^{-3}

27. $(-a)^{-4}$

28. $-b^{-3}$

29. $4a^{-3}$

30. $2b^{-2}$

31. $(3a)^{-2}$

32. $(-b)^{-2}$

33. $2a^{-1}b^{-2}$

34. $-4a^{-2}b^{-3}$

35. $3^{-2}a^{-2}b^{-1}$

36. $(3ab)^{-2}$

Simplify each expression.

37. x^{-8}

38. xy^{-3}

39. $a^{-5}b$

40. m^2n^{-9}

41. $\dfrac{1}{x^{-7}}$

42. $\dfrac{3}{a^{-4}}$

43. $\dfrac{5}{d^{-3}}$

44. $\dfrac{6}{r^{-5}s^{-1}}$

45. $3x^{-6}y^{-5}$

46. $8a^{-3}b^2c^{-2}$

47. $15s^{-9}t^{-1}$

48. $-7p^{-5}q^{-3}r^2$

49. $\dfrac{d^{-4}}{e^{-7}}$

50. $\dfrac{3m^{-4}}{n^{-8}}$

51. $\dfrac{6m^{-8}n}{p^{-1}}$

52. $\dfrac{a^{-2}b^{-1}}{cd^{-3}}$

Write each number as a power of 10 using a negative exponent.

53. $\dfrac{1}{10,000}$

54. $\dfrac{1}{1,000,000}$

55. $\dfrac{1}{10,000,000}$

56. $\dfrac{1}{1,000,000,000}$

Write each expression as a decimal.

57. 10^{-5}

58. 10^{-8}

59. $4 \cdot 10^{-1}$

60. $6 \cdot 10^{-4}$

Evaluate each expression for $m = 4$, $n = 5$, and $p = -2$.

61. m^p

62. n^m

63. p^p

64. n^p

65. $m^p n$

66. m^{-n}

67. p^{-n}

68. mn^p

69. p^{-m}

70. $\dfrac{m}{n^p}$

71. $\dfrac{1}{n^{-m}}$

72. $-n^{-m}$

Practice 8-2

Write each number in standard notation.

1. 7×10^4 **2.** 3×10^{-2} **3.** 2.6×10^5 **4.** 7.1×10^{-4}

5. 5.71×10^{-5} **6.** 4.155×10^7 **7.** 3.0107×10^2 **8.** 9.407×10^{-5}

9. 31.3×10^6 **10.** 83.7×10^{-4} **11.** 0.018×10^{-1} **12.** 0.016×10^5

13. 8.0023×10^{-3} **14.** 6.902×10^8 **15.** 1005×10^2 **16.** 0.095×10^{-1}

Write each number in scientific notation.

17. 51,000,000   **18.** 975,000,000,000   **19.** 0.00000012   **20.** 0.000005008

21. 1560 billion   **22.** 0.5 million   **23.** 2 thousandths   **24.** 1095 millionths

25. 194×10^3 **26.** 154×10^{-3} **27.** 0.05×10^6 **28.** 0.031×10^{-4}

29. 790 thousand   **30.** 25 hundredths   **31.** 0.000000000159   **32.** 5,000,900,000,000

Order the numbers in each list from least to greatest.

33. $7 \times 10^{-7}, 6 \times 10^{-8}, 5 \times 10^{-6}, 4 \times 10^{-10}$

34. $5.01 \times 10^{-4}, 4.8 \times 10^{-3}, 5.2 \times 10^{-2}, 5.6 \times 10^{-2}$

35. $62,040, 6.2 \times 10^2, 6.207 \times 10^3, 6.34 \times 10^{-1}$

36. $10^{-3}, 5 \times 10^{-3}, 8 \times 10^{-2}, 4 \times 10^{-1}$

Simplify. Write each answer using scientific notation.

37. $4(3 \times 10^5)$ **38.** $5(7 \times 10^{-2})$ **39.** $8(9 \times 10^9)$

40. $7(9 \times 10^6)$ **41.** $3(1.2 \times 10^{-4})$ **42.** $2(6.1 \times 10^{-8})$

43. $3(1.2 \times 10^{-4})$ **44.** $3(4.3 \times 10^{-4})$ **45.** $3(3.2 \times 10^{-2})$

Complete the table.

Units of Area in Square Feet		
Unit	Standard Form	Scientific Notation
46. 1 in.^{2} =		6.9444×10^{-3}
47. 1 link^2 =	0.4356	
48. 1 rod^2 =	272.25	
49. 1 mi^2 =		2.78×10^7
50. 1 cm^2 =	0.001076	
51. 1 hectare =		1.08×10^7

Practice 8-3

Simplify each expression.

1. $(3d^{-4})(5d^8)$

2. $(-8m^4)(4m^8)$

3. $n^{-6} \cdot n^{-9}$

4. $a^3 \cdot a$

5. $3^8 \cdot 3^5$

6. $(3p^{-15})(6p^{11})$

7. $p^7 \cdot q^5 \cdot p^6$

8. $(-1.5a^5b^2)(6a)$

9. $(-2d^3e^3)(6d^4e^6)$

10. $\dfrac{1}{b^{-7} \cdot b^5}$

11. $p^5 \cdot q^2 \cdot p^4$

12. $\dfrac{1}{n^7 \cdot n^{-5}}$

13. $(8d^4)(4d^7)$

14. $x^{-9} \cdot x^3 \cdot x^2$

15. $2^3 \cdot 2^2$

16. $r^7 \cdot s^4 \cdot s \cdot r^3$

17. $b^7 \cdot b^{13}$

18. $(7p^4)(5p^9)$

19. $2^8 \cdot 2^{-9} \cdot 2^3$

20. $(6r^4s^3)(9rs^2)$

21. $4^3 \cdot 4^2$

22. $m^{12} \cdot m^{-14}$

23. $s^7 \cdot t^4 \cdot t^8$

24. $(-3xy^6)(3.2x^5y)$

25. $5^{-7} \cdot 5^9$

26. $\dfrac{1}{h^7 \cdot h^3}$

27. $\dfrac{1}{t^{-5} \cdot t^{-3}}$

28. $f^5 \cdot f^2 \cdot f^0$

29. $r^6 \cdot r^{-13}$

30. $5^{-6} \cdot 5^4$

Simplify each expression. Write each answer in scientific notation.

31. $(7 \times 10^7)(5 \times 10^{-5})$

32. $(3 \times 10^8)(3 \times 10^4)$

33. $(9.5 \times 10^{-4})(2 \times 10^{-5})$

34. $(4 \times 10^9)(4.1 \times 10^8)$

35. $(7.2 \times 10^{-7})(2 \times 10^{-5})$

36. $(5 \times 10^7)(4 \times 10^3)$

37. $(6 \times 10^{-6})(5.2 \times 10^4)$

38. $(4 \times 10^6)(9 \times 10^8)$

39. $(6.1 \times 10^9)(8 \times 10^{14})$

40. $(2.1 \times 10^{-4})(4 \times 10^{-7})$

41. $(1.6 \times 10^5)(3 \times 10^{11})$

42. $(9 \times 10^{12})(0.3 \times 10^{-18})$

43. $(4 \times 10^9)(11 \times 10^3)$

44. $(5 \times 10^{13})(9 \times 10^{-9})$

45. $(7 \times 10^6)(4 \times 10^9)$

46. $(6 \times 10^{-8})(12 \times 10^{-7})$

47. $(6 \times 10^{15})(3.2 \times 10^2)$

48. $(5 \times 10^8)(2.6 \times 10^{-16})$

49. In 1990, the St. Louis metropolitan area had an average of 82×10^{-6} g/m^3 of pollutants in the air. How many grams of pollutants were there in 2×10^3 m^3 of air?

50. Light travels approximately 5.87×10^{12} mi in one year. This distance is called a light-year. Suppose a star is 2×10^4 light-years away. How many miles away is that star?

51. The weight of 1 m^3 of air is approximately 1.3×10^3 g. Suppose that the volume of air inside of a building is 3×10^6 m^3. How much does the air inside the building weigh?

52. Light travels 1.18×10^{10} in. in 1 second. How far will light travel in 1 nanosecond or 1×10^{-9} s?

Practice 8-4

More Multiplication Properties of Exponents

Simplify each expression.

1. $(4a^5)^3$

2. $(2^{-3})^4$

3. $(m^{-3}n^4)^{-4}$

4. $(x^5)^2$

5. $2^5 \cdot (2^4)^2$

6. $(4x^4)^3(2xy^3)^2$

7. $x^4 \cdot (x^4)^3$

8. $(x^5y^3)^3(xy^5)^2$

9. $(5^2)^2$

10. $(a^4)^{-5} \cdot a^{13}$

11. $(3f^4g^{-3})^3(f^2g^{-2})^{-1}$

12. $x^3 \cdot (x^3)^5$

13. $(d^2)^{-4}$

14. $(a^3b^4)^{-2}(a^{-3}b^{-5})^{-4}$

15. $(x^2y)^4$

16. $(12b^{-2})^2$

17. $(m^{-5})^{-3}$

18. $(x^{-4})^5(x^3y^2)^5$

19. $(y^6)^{-3} \cdot y^{21}$

20. $n^6 \cdot (n^{-2})^5$

21. $(m^5)^{-3}(m^4n^5)^4$

22. $(a^3)^6$

23. $b^{-9} \cdot (b^2)^4$

24. $(4^{-1}s^3)^{-2}$

25. $(5a^3b^5)^4$

26. $(b^{-3})^6$

27. $(y^6)^3$

28. $a^{-4} \cdot (a^4b^3)^2$

29. $(x^4y)^3$

30. $d^3 \cdot (d^2)^5$

Simplify. Write each answer in scientific notation.

31. $10^{-9} \cdot (2 \times 10^2)^2$

32. $(3 \times 10^{-6})^3$

33. $10^4 \cdot (4 \times 10^6)^3$

34. $(9 \times 10^7)^2$

35. $10^{-3} \cdot (2 \times 10^3)^5$

36. $(7 \times 10^5)^3$

37. $(5 \times 10^5)^4$

38. $(2 \times 10^{-3})^3$

39. $(5 \times 10^2)^{-3}$

40. $(3 \times 10^5)^4$

41. $(4 \times 10^8)^{-3}$

42. $(1 \times 10^{-5})^{-5}$

43. $10^5 \cdot (8 \times 10^7)^3$

44. $(10^2)^3(6 \times 10^{-3})^3$

45. $10^7 \cdot (2 \times 10^2)^4$

46. The kinetic energy, in joules, of a moving object is found by using the formula $E = \frac{1}{2}mv^2$, where m is the mass and v is the speed of the object. The mass of a car is 1.59×10^3 kg. The car is traveling at 2.7×10^1 m/s. What is the kinetic energy of the car?

47. The moon is shaped somewhat like a sphere. The surface area of the moon is found by using the formula $S = 12.56r^2$. What is the surface area of the moon if the radius is 1.08×10^3 mi?

48. Because of a record corn harvest, excess corn is stored on the ground in a pile. The pile is shaped like a cone. The height of the pile is 25 ft, and the radius of the pile is 1.2×10^2 ft. Use the formula $V = \frac{1}{3}\pi r^2h$ to find the volume.

49. Suppose the distance in feet that an object travels in t seconds is given by the formula $d = 64t^2$. How far would the object travel after 1.5×10^3 seconds?

Practice 8-5

Simplify each expression.

1. $\dfrac{c^{15}}{c^9}$

2. $\left(\dfrac{x^3 y^{-2}}{z^{-5}}\right)^{-4}$

3. $\dfrac{x^7 y^9 z^3}{x^4 y^7 z^8}$

4. $\left(\dfrac{a^2}{b^3}\right)^5$

5. $\dfrac{3^7}{3^4}$

6. $\left(\dfrac{a^3}{b^2}\right)^4$

7. $\left(\dfrac{2}{3}\right)^{-2}$

8. $\left(\dfrac{p^{-3} q^{-2}}{q^{-3} r^5}\right)^4$

9. $\dfrac{a^6 b^{-5}}{a^{-2} b^7}$

10. $\dfrac{7^{-4}}{7^{-7}}$

11. $\dfrac{a^7 b^6}{a^5 b}$

12. $\left(\dfrac{a^2 b^{-4}}{b^2}\right)^5$

13. $\left(-\dfrac{3}{2^3}\right)^{-2}$

14. $\dfrac{z^7}{z^{-3}}$

15. $\left(\dfrac{5 a^0 b^4}{c^{-3}}\right)^2$

16. $\dfrac{x^4 y^{-8} z^{-2}}{x^{-1} y^6 z^{-10}}$

17. $\dfrac{m^6}{m^{10}}$

18. $\left(\dfrac{2^3 m^4 n^{-1}}{p^2}\right)^0$

19. $\left(\dfrac{s^{-4}}{t^{-1}}\right)^{-2}$

20. $\left(\dfrac{2 a^3 b^{-2}}{c^3}\right)^5$

21. $\left(\dfrac{x^{-3} y}{xz^{-4}}\right)^{-2}$

22. $\dfrac{h^{-13}}{h^{-8}}$

23. $\dfrac{4^6}{4^8}$

24. $\left(\dfrac{1}{3}\right)^3$

25. $\dfrac{x^5 y^3}{x^2 y^9}$

26. $\left(\dfrac{m^{-3} n^4}{n^{-2}}\right)^4$

27. $\dfrac{4^{-1}}{4^2}$

28. $\left(\dfrac{a^8 b^6}{a^{11}}\right)^5$

29. $\dfrac{n^9}{n^{15}}$

30. $\left(\dfrac{r^3 s^{-1}}{r^2 s^6}\right)^{-1}$

31. $\dfrac{n^{-8}}{n^4}$

32. $\dfrac{m^8 n^3}{m^{10} n^5}$

Simplify each quotient. Write each answer in scientific notation.

33. $\dfrac{3.54 \times 10^{-9}}{6.15 \times 10^{-5}}$

34. $\dfrac{9.35 \times 10^{-3}}{3.71 \times 10^{-5}}$

35. $\dfrac{495 \text{ billion}}{23.9 \text{ million}}$

36. $\dfrac{8 \times 10^9}{4 \times 10^5}$

37. $\dfrac{9.5 \times 10^9}{5 \times 10^{12}}$

38. $\dfrac{6.4 \times 10^9}{8 \times 10^7}$

39. $\dfrac{298 \text{ billion}}{49 \text{ million}}$

40. $\dfrac{1.8 \times 10^{-8}}{0.9 \times 10^3}$

41. $\dfrac{3.6 \times 10^6}{9 \times 10^{-3}}$

42. $\dfrac{8.19 \times 10^7}{4.76 \times 10^{-2}}$

43. $\dfrac{65 \text{ million}}{19.5 \text{ billion}}$

44. $\dfrac{4.9 \times 10^{12}}{7 \times 10^3}$

45. $\dfrac{36.2 \text{ trillion}}{98.5 \text{ billion}}$

46. $\dfrac{3.9 \times 10^3}{1.3 \times 10^8}$

47. $\dfrac{5.6 \times 10^{-5}}{8 \times 10^{-7}}$

48. $\dfrac{40 \text{ million}}{985 \text{ million}}$

49. The half-life of uranium-238 is 4.5×10^9 years. The half-life of uranium-234 is 2.5×10^5 years. How many times greater is the half-life of uranium-238 than that of uranium-234.

Practice 8-6

Find the next three terms of each sequence.

1. $4, 12, 36, 108, \ldots$

2. $2, -8, 32, -128, \ldots$

3. $18, 9, \frac{9}{2}, \frac{9}{4}, \ldots$

4. $1, -\frac{1}{3}, \frac{1}{9}, -\frac{1}{27}, \ldots$

5. $-2, 20, -200, 2000, \ldots$

6. $30, -10, \frac{10}{3}, -\frac{10}{9}, \ldots$

7. $\frac{1}{3}, 1\frac{1}{3}, 5\frac{1}{3}, 21\frac{1}{3}, \ldots$

8. $20, 4, \frac{4}{5}, \frac{4}{25}, \ldots$

9. $-100, -40, -16, -6.4, \ldots$

10. $40, 20, 10, 5, \ldots$

Determine whether each sequence is arithmetic or geometric.

11. $-8, -10, -12.5, -15.625, \ldots$

12. $5, 1, -3, -7, \ldots$

13. $1, \frac{2}{5}, \frac{4}{25}, \frac{8}{125}, \ldots$

14. $-0.2, -0.02, -0.002, -0.0002, \ldots$

15. $-10, -5, 0, 5, \ldots$

16. $6, -3, \frac{3}{2}, -\frac{3}{4}, \ldots$

Write a rule for each sequence.

17. $4, 12, 36, 108, \ldots$

18. $2, -8, 32, -128, \ldots$

19. $18, 9, \frac{9}{2}, \frac{9}{4}, \ldots$

20. $1, -\frac{1}{3}, \frac{1}{9}, -\frac{1}{27}, \ldots$

21. $-2, 20, -200, 2000, \ldots$

22. $30, -10, \frac{10}{3}, -\frac{10}{9}, \ldots$

23. $1, 4, 16, 64, \ldots$

24. $6, 12, 24, 48, \ldots$

25. $125, 25, 5, 1, \ldots$

26. $50, 25, 12.5, 6.25, \ldots$

Find the first, fourth, and eighth terms of each sequence.

27. $A(n) = 2 \cdot 3^{n-1}$

28. $A(n) = 3 \cdot 4^{n-1}$

29. $A(n) = 3 \cdot 2^{n-1}$

30. $A(n) = -1 \cdot 5^{n-1}$

31. $A(n) = 4 \cdot 2^{n-1}$

32. $A(n) = \frac{1}{2} \cdot 2^{n-1}$

33. $A(n) = 0.1 \cdot 4^{n-1}$

34. $A(n) = -2.1 \cdot 3^{n-1}$

35. $A(n) = 10 \cdot 5^{n-1}$

Write a rule and find the given term in each geometric sequence described below.

36. What is the sixth term when the first term is 4 and the common ratio is 3?

37. What is the fifth term when the first term is -2 and the common ratio is $-\frac{1}{2}$?

38. What is the tenth term when the first term is 3 and the common ratio is -1.2?

39. What is the fourth term when the first term is 5 and the common ratio is 6?

40. Suppose a manufacturer invented a computer chip in 1978 that had a computational speed of *s*. The company improves its chips so that every 3 years, the chip doubles in speed. What would the chip's speed have been for the year 2002? Write your solution in terms of *s*.

Name _____ Class _____ Date _____

Practice 8-7

Exponential Functions

Complete the table for each exercise.

1. Investment increases by 1.5 times every 5 yr.

Time	Value of Investment
Initial	$800
5 yr	$1200
10 yr	$1800
15 yr	$2700
20 yr	■
25 yr	■
■	■
■	■

2. The number of animals doubles every 3 mo.

Time	Number of Animals
Initial	18
3 mo	36
6 mo	72
9 mo	■
12 mo	■
■	■
■	■

3. The amount of matter halves every year.

Time	Amount of Matter
Initial	3200 g
1 yr	1600 g
2 yr	800 g
3 yr	■
■	■
■	■
■	■

Evaluate each function for the domain {–2, 0, 1, 2, 4}.

4. $y = 2^x$

5. $y = 3.1^x$

6. $y = 0.8^x$

7. $y = 2 \cdot 4^x$

8. $y = 10 \cdot 3^x$

9. $y = 25 \cdot 5^x$

10. $y = \left(\frac{2}{3}\right)^x$

11. $y = 100 \cdot \left(\frac{1}{10}\right)^x$

12. $y = \frac{1}{4} \cdot 8^x$

Graph each function.

13. $y = 3^x$

14. $y = 6^x$

15. $y = 1.5^x$

16. $y = 7^x$

17. $y = 10 \cdot 5^x$

18. $y = 16 \cdot 0.5^x$

19. $y = \frac{1}{8} \cdot 2^x$

20. $y = \frac{1}{2} \cdot 4^x$

21. $y = 8 \cdot \left(\frac{5}{2}\right)^x$

Evaluate each function rule for the given values.

22. $y = 5.5^x$ for $x = 1, 3,$ and 4

23. $y = 4 \cdot 1.5^x$ for $x = 2, 4,$ and 5

24. $y = 3 \cdot 4^x$ for $x = 1, 3,$ and 5

25. $y = 6^x$ for $x = 2, 3,$ and 4

26. $y = 0.7^x$ for $x = 1, 3,$ and 4

27. $y = 3.1^x$ for $x = 1, 2,$ and 3

28. $y = 180 \cdot 0.5^x$ for $x = 0, -2,$ and $-\frac{1}{2}$

29. $y = 4.3^x$ for $x = -2, -1,$ and 0

30. $y = 100 \cdot 0.1^x$ for $x = -4, -1,$ and 2

31. $y = 5^x$ for $x = -2, -3,$ and 4

Solve each equation.

32. $5^x = 625$

33. $2 \cdot 4^x = 128$

34. $4^x = \frac{1}{64}$

35. $4 \cdot 5^x = \frac{4}{125}$

Practice 8-8

Write an exponential function to model each situation. Find each amount after the specified time.

1. Suppose one of your ancestors invested $500 in 1800 in an account paying 4% interest compounded annually. Find the account balance in each of the following years.

   a. 1850   **b.** 1900   **c.** 2000   **d.** 2100

2. Suppose you invest $1500 in an account paying 4.75% annual interest. Find the account balance after 25 yr with the interest compounded the following ways.

   a. annually   **b.** semiannually   **c.** quarterly   **d.** monthly

3. The starting salary for a new employee is $25,000. The salary for this employee increases by 8% per year. What is the salary after each of the following?

   a. 1 yr   **b.** 3 yr   **c.** 5 yr   **d.** 15 yr

4. Carbon-14 has a half-life of 5,700 years. Scientists use this fact to determine the age of things made of organic material. Suppose the average page of a book containing approximately 0.5 mg of carbon-14 is put into a time capsule. How much carbon-14 will each page contain after each of the following numbers of years?

   a. 5700   **b.** 11,400   **c.** 22,800   **d.** 34,200

5. The tax revenue that a small city receives increases by 3.5% per year. In 1990, the city received $250,000 in tax revenue. Determine the tax revenue in each of the following years.

   a. 1995   **b.** 1998   **c.** 2000   **d.** 2006

6. Suppose the acreage of forest is decreasing by 2% per year because of development. If there are currently 4,500,000 acres of forest, determine the amount of forest land after each of the following.

   a. 3 yr   **b.** 5 yr   **c.** 10 yr   **d.** 20 yr

7. A $10,500 investment has a 15% loss each year. Determine the value of the investment after each of the following.

   a. 1 yr   **b.** 2 yr   **c.** 4 yr   **d.** 10 yr

8. A city of 2,950,000 people has a 2.5% annual decrease in population. Determine the city's population after each of the following.

   a. 1 yr   **b.** 5 yr   **c.** 15 yr   **d.** 25 yr

9. A $25,000 purchase decreases 12% in value per year. Determine the value of the purchase after each of the following.

   a. 1 yr   **b.** 3 yr   **c.** 5 yr   **d.** 7 yr

Practice 9-1

Write each polynomial in standard form. Then name each polynomial based on its degree and number of terms.

1. $4y^3 - 4y^2 + 3 - y$

2. $x^2 + x^4 - 6$

3. $x + 2$

4. $2m^2 - 7m^3 + 3m$

5. $4 - x + 2x^2$

6. $7x^3 + 2x^2$

7. $n^2 - 5n$

8. $6 + 7x^2$

9. $3a^2 + a^3 - 4a + 3$

10. $5 + 3x$

11. $7 - 8a^2 + 6a$

12. $5x + 4 - x^2$

13. $2 + 4x^2 - x^3$

14. $4x^3 - 2x^2$

15. $y^2 - 7 - 3y$

16. $x - 6x^2 - 3$

17. $v^3 - v + 2v^2$

18. $8d + 3d^2$

Simplify. Write each answer in standard form.

19. $(3x^2 - 5x) - (x^2 + 4x + 3)$

20. $(2x^3 - 4x^2 + 3) + (x^3 - 3x^2 + 1)$

21. $(3y^3 - 11y + 3) - (5y^3 + y^2 + 2)$

22. $(3x^2 + 2x^3) - (3x^2 + 7x - 1)$

23. $(2a^3 + 3a^2 + 7a) + (a^3 + a^2 - 2a)$

24. $(8y^3 - y + 7) - (6y^3 + 3y - 3)$

25. $(x^2 - 6) + (5x^2 + x - 3)$

26. $(5n^2 - 7) - (2n^2 + n - 3)$

27. $(5n^3 + 2n^2 + 2) - (n^3 + 3n^2 - 2)$

28. $(3y^2 - 7y + 3) - (5y + 3 - 4y^2)$

29. $(2x^2 + 9x - 17) + (x^2 - 6x - 3)$

30. $(3 - x^3 - 5x^2) + (x + 2x^3 - 3)$

31. $(3x + x^2 - x^3) - (x^3 + 2x^2 + 5x)$

32. $(d^2 + 8 - 5d) - (5d^2 + d - 2d^3 + 3)$

33. $(3x^3 + 7x^2) + (x^2 - 2x^3)$

34. $(6c^2 + 5c - 3) - (3c^2 + 8c)$

35. $(3y^2 - 5y - 7) + (y^2 - 6y + 7)$

36. $(3c^2 - 8c + 4) - (7 + c^2 - 8c)$

37. $(4x^2 + 13x + 9) + (12x^2 + x + 6)$

38. $(2x - 13x^2 + 3) - (2x^2 + 8x)$

39. $(7x - 4x^2 + 11) + (7x^2 + 5)$

40. $(4x + 7x^3 - 9x^2) + (3 - 2x^2 - 5x)$

41. $(y^3 + y^2 - 2) + (y - 6y^2)$

42. $(x^2 - 8x - 3) - (x^3 + 8x^2 - 8)$

43. $(3x^2 - 2x + 9) - (x^2 - x + 7)$

44. $(2x^2 - 6x + 3) - (2x + 4x^2 + 2)$

45. $(2x^2 - 2x^3 - 7) + (9x^2 + 2 + x)$

46. $(3a^2 + a^3 - 1) + (2a^2 + 3a + 1)$

47. $(2x^2 + 3 - x) - (2 + 2x^2 - 5x)$

48. $(n^4 - 2n - 1) + (5n - n^4 + 5)$

49. $(x^3 + 3x) - (x^2 + 6 - 4x)$

50. $(7s^2 + 4s + 2) + (3s + 2 - s^2)$

51. $(6x^2 - 3x + 9) - (x^2 + 3x - 5)$

52. $(3x^3 - x^2 + 4) + (2x^3 - 3x + 9)$

53. $(y^3 + 3y - 1) - (y^3 + 3y + 5)$

54. $(3 + 5x^3 + 2x) - (x + 2x^2 + 4x^3)$

55. $(x^2 + 15x + 13) + (3x^2 - 15x + 7)$

56. $(7 - 8x^2) + (x^3 - x + 5)$

57. $(2x + 3) - (x - 4) + (x + 2)$

58. $(x^2 + 4) - (x - 4) + (x^2 - 2x)$

Practice 9-2

Simplify each product.

1. $4(a - 3)$ **2.** $-5(x - 2)$ **3.** $-3x^2(x^2 + 3x)$

4. $4x^3(x - 3)$ **5.** $-5x^2(x^2 + 2x + 1)$ **6.** $3x(x^2 - 5x - 3)$

7. $-x^2(-2x^2 + 3x - 2)$ **8.** $4d^2(d^2 - 3d - 7)$ **9.** $5m^3(m + 6)$

10. $a^2(2a + 4)$ **11.** $4(x^2 - 3) + x(x + 1)$ **12.** $4x(5x - 6)$

Find the GCF of the terms of each polynomial.

13. $8x - 4$ **14.** $15x + 45x^2$ **15.** $x^2 + 3x$

16. $4c^3 - 8c^2 + 8$ **17.** $12x - 36$ **18.** $12n^3 + 4n^2$

19. $14x^3 + 7x^2$ **20.** $8x^3 - 12x$ **21.** $9 - 27x^3$

22. $25x^3 - 15x^2$ **23.** $11x^2 - 33x$ **24.** $4n^4 + 6n^3 - 8n^2$

25. $8d^3 + 4d^2 + 12d$ **26.** $6x^2 + 12x - 21$ **27.** $8g^2 + 16g - 8$

Factor each polynomial.

28. $8x + 10$ **29.** $12n^3 - 8n$ **30.** $14d - 2$

31. $6h^2 - 8h$ **32.** $3z^4 - 15z^3 - 9z^2$ **33.** $3y^3 - 8y^2 - 9y$

34. $x^3 - 5x^2$ **35.** $8x^3 - 12x^2 + 4x$ **36.** $7x^3 + 21x^4$

37. $6a^3 - 12a^2 + 14a$ **38.** $6x^4 + 12x^2$ **39.** $3n^4 - 6n^2 + 9n$

40. $2w^3 + 6w^2 - 4w$ **41.** $12c^3 - 30c^2$ **42.** $2x^2 + 8x - 14$

43. $4x^3 + 12x^2 + 16x$ **44.** $16m^3 - 8m^2 + 12m$ **45.** $4a^3 - 20a^2 - 8a$

46. $18c^4 - 9c^2 + 7c$ **47.** $6y^4 + 9y^3 - 27y^2$ **48.** $6c^2 - 3c$

49. A circular pond will be placed on a square piece of land. The length of a side of the square is $2x$. The radius of the pond is x. The part of the square not covered by the pond will be planted with flowers. What is the area of the region that will be planted with flowers? Write your answer in factored form.

50. A square poster of length $3x$ is to have a square painting centered on it. The length of the painting is $2x$. The area of the poster not covered by the painting will be painted black. What is the area of the poster that will be painted black?

51. The formula for the surface area of a sphere is $A = 4\pi r^2$. A square sticker of side x is placed on a ball of radius $3x$. What is the surface area of the sphere not covered by the sticker? Write your answer in factored form.

Practice 9-3

Simplify each product. Write in standard form.

1. $(x + 3)(2x - 5)$ **2.** $(x^2 + x - 1)(x + 1)$ **3.** $(3w + 4)(2w - 1)$

4. $(x + 5)(x + 4)$ **5.** $(2b - 1)(b^2 - 3b + 4)$ **6.** $(a - 11)(a + 5)$

7. $(2g - 3)(2g^2 + g - 4)$ **8.** $(3s - 4)(s - 5)$ **9.** $(4x + 3)(x - 7)$

10. $(x + 6)(x^2 - 4x + 3)$ **11.** $(5x - 3)(4x + 2)$ **12.** $(3y + 7)(4y + 5)$

13. $(3x + 7)(x + 5)$ **14.** $(5x - 2)(x + 3)$ **15.** $(3m^2 - 7m + 8)(m - 2)$

16. $(a - 6)(a + 8)$ **17.** $(x + 2)(2x^2 - 3x + 2)$ **18.** $(a^2 + a + 1)(a - 1)$

19. $(x - 2)(x^2 + 4x + 4)$ **20.** $(2r + 1)(3r - 1)$ **21.** $(k + 4)(3k - 4)$

22. $(2n - 3)(n^2 - 2n + 5)$ **23.** $(p - 4)(2p + 3)$ **24.** $(3x + 1)(4x^2 - 2x + 1)$

25. $(2x^2 - 5x + 2)(4x - 3)$ **26.** $(x + 7)(x + 5)$ **27.** $(6x - 11)(x + 2)$

28. $(2x + 1)(4x + 3)$ **29.** $(3x + 4)(3x - 4)$ **30.** $(6x - 5)(3x + 1)$

31. $(n - 7)(n + 4)$ **32.** $(3x - 1)(2x + 1)$ **33.** $(d + 9)(d - 11)$

34. $(2x^2 + 5x - 3)(2x + 1)$ **35.** $(b + 8)(2b - 5)$ **36.** $(2x - 5)(x + 4)$

37. $(3x + 5)(5x - 7)$ **38.** $(x - 5)(2x^2 - 7x - 2)$ **39.** $(2x^2 - 9x + 11)(2x + 1)$

40. $(2x^2 + 5x - 4)(2x + 7)$ **41.** $(x^2 + 6x + 11)(3x + 5)$ **42.** $(5x + 7)(7x + 3)$

43. $(4x - 7)(2x - 5)$ **44.** $(x - 9)(3x + 5)$ **45.** $(2x - 1)(x^2 - 7x + 1)$

46. The width of a rectangular painting is 3 in. more than twice the height.
A frame that is 2.5 in. wide goes around the painting.

  a. Write an expression for the combined area of the painting
  and frame.

  b. Use the expression to find the combined area when the height of
  the painting is 12 in.

  c. Use the expression to find the combined area when the height of
  the painting is 15 in.

47. The Robertsons put a rectangular pool with a stone walkway around it
in their backyard. The total length of the pool and walkway is 3 times
the total width. The walkway is 2 ft wide all around.

  a. Write an expression for the area of the pool.

  b. Find the area of the pool when the total width is 10 ft.

  c. Find the area of the pool when the total width is 9 ft.

48. The Cutting Edge frame shop makes a mat by cutting out the
inside of a rectangular board. Use the diagram to find the
length and width of the original board if the area of the mat
is 184 in.^{2}.

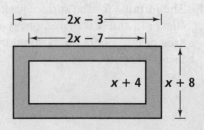

Practice 9-4

Simplify.

1. $(w - 2)^2$

2. $(y + 4)^2$

3. $(4w + 2)^2$

4. $(w - 9)^2$

5. $(3x + 7)^2$

6. $(3x - 7)^2$

7. $(2x - 9)^2$

8. $(x - 12)^2$

9. $(6x + 1)^2$

10. $(4x - 7)^2$

11. $(x + 8)(x - 8)$

12. $(x - 11)(x + 11)$

13. $(x - 12)(x + 12)$

14. $(y + w)(y - w)$

15. $(2x + 1)(2x - 1)$

16. $(5x - 2)(5x + 2)$

17. $(6x + 1)(6x - 1)$

18. $(2x - 4)(2x + 4)$

19. $(x^2 + y^2)^2$

20. $(2x^2 + y^2)^2$

21. $(a^2 - b^2)^2$

22. $(y^2 - 4w^2)^2$

23. $(3 - 6x^2)^2$

24. $(4a - 3y)^2$

25. $(3y + 2a)(3y - 2a)$

26. $(x^2 + 2y)(x^2 - 2y)$

27. $(3x^2 + 4w^2)(3x^2 - 4w^2)$

28. $(4x + 3w^2)(4x - 3w^2)$

29. $(2a + 7b)(2a - 7b)$

30. $(5a^2 - 6x)(5a^2 + 6x)$

31. 18^2

32. $(64)^2$

33. $(29)(31)$

34. $(97)(103)$

35. $(19)(42)$

36. $(95)(205)$

Find the area.

37.

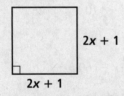

2x + 1

2x + 1

38.

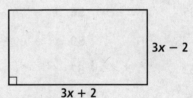

3x − 2

3x + 2

Find the area of the shaded region.

39.

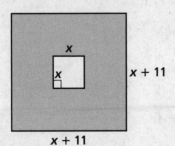

x

x

x + 11

x + 11

40.

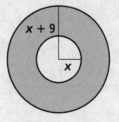

x + 9

x

Practice 9-5

Factoring Trinomials of the Type $x^2 + bx + c$

Factor each expression.

1. $x^2 + 8x + 16$

2. $d^2 + 8d + 7$

3. $y^2 + 6y + 8$

4. $b^2 - 2b - 3$

5. $s^2 - 4s - 5$

6. $x^2 + 12x + 32$

7. $x^2 - 9x + 20$

8. $x^2 - 5x + 6$

9. $a^2 + 3a + 2$

10. $p^2 - 8p + 7$

11. $d^2 + 6d + 5$

12. $n^2 + n - 6$

13. $x^2 + 5x - 14$

14. $b^2 + 9b + 14$

15. $x^2 + 14x + 45$

16. $a^2 + 7a + 12$

17. $x^2 + 13x + 22$

18. $x^2 + 3x - 4$

19. $x^2 - 8x + 12$

20. $x^2 + 7x - 18$

21. $n^2 - 7n + 10$

22. $s^2 - 5s - 14$

23. $x^2 - 9x + 8$

24. $x^2 - 2x - 24$

25. $x^2 - 6x - 27$

26. $x^2 - 16x - 36$

27. $x^2 + 7x + 10$

28. $x^2 - 3x - 28$

29. $m^2 - 4m - 21$

30. $x^2 - 2x - 15$

31. $x^2 - 5x - 24$

32. $b^2 - 4b - 60$

33. $x^2 - 3x - 18$

34. $m^2 + 7m + 10$

35. $n^2 - n - 72$

36. $k^2 - 6k + 5$

37. $x^2 + 9x + 20$

38. $x^2 - 10x + 9$

39. $x^2 - 8x + 16$

40. $d^2 - 4d + 3$

41. $b^2 - 26b + 48$

42. $n^2 - 15n + 26$

43. $n^2 - n - 6$

44. $z^2 - 14z + 49$

45. $x^2 + 7x + 12$

46. $x^2 - 18x + 17$

47. $x^2 + 16x + 28$

48. $t^2 - 6t - 27$

49. $b^2 + 4b - 12$

50. $d^2 + 11d + 18$

51. $x^2 + x - 20$

52. $x^2 - 13x + 42$

53. $x^2 + x - 6$

54. $x^2 + 4x - 21$

55. $a^2 + 2a - 35$

56. $h^2 + 7h - 18$

57. $x^2 + 3x - 10$

58. $p^2 - 12p - 28$

59. $y^2 + 6y - 55$

60. $b^2 + 3b - 4$

61. $x^2 + 2x - 63$

62. $x^2 - 2x - 8$

63. $x^2 - 11x - 60$

64. $r^2 + 2r - 35$

65. $c^2 - 3c - 10$

66. $x^2 + 8x + 15$

67. $x^2 - 8x + 15$

68. $n^2 - 23n + 60$

69. $c^2 + 3c - 10$

70. $x^2 - 9x + 14$

71. $x^2 - 10x + 24$

72. $x^2 + 6x - 27$

73. $y^2 - 16y + 64$

74. $n^2 + 10n + 25$

75. $r^2 - 14r - 51$

76. $x^2 + 3x - 40$

77. $x^2 - x - 42$

78. $n^2 - 2n - 63$

79. $a^2 + 7a + 6$

80. $x^2 - 14x + 48$

81. $x^2 - 11x + 28$

82. $n^2 + 16n - 36$

83. $n^2 - 4n - 21$

84. $y^2 + 16y - 17$

Practice 9-6

Factor each expression.

1. $2x^2 + 3x + 1$

2. $2x^2 + 5x + 3$

3. $2n^2 + n - 6$

4. $3x^2 - x - 4$

5. $2y^2 - 9y - 5$

6. $5x^2 - 2x - 7$

7. $7n^2 + 9n + 2$

8. $3c^2 - 17c - 6$

9. $3x^2 + 8x + 4$

10. $6x^2 - 7x - 10$

11. $3x^2 - 10x + 8$

12. $3y^2 - 16y - 12$

13. $5x^2 + 2x - 3$

14. $3x^2 + 7x + 2$

15. $7x^2 - 10x + 3$

16. $3x^2 + 8x + 5$

17. $2x^2 + 9x + 4$

18. $5x^2 - 7x + 2$

19. $5x^2 - 22x + 8$

20. $4x^2 + 17x - 15$

21. $5x^2 - 33x - 14$

22. $3x^2 - 2x - 8$

23. $3y^2 + 7y - 6$

24. $2x^2 + 13x - 24$

25. $4y^2 - 11y - 3$

26. $2y^2 + 9y + 7$

27. $5y^2 - 3y - 2$

28. $7y^2 + 19y + 10$

29. $7x^2 - 30x + 8$

30. $3x^2 + 17x + 10$

31. $2x^2 + 5x - 3$

32. $2x^2 - 5x + 3$

33. $3x^2 + 10x + 3$

34. $2x^2 - x - 21$

35. $5x^2 - 11x + 2$

36. $4x^2 + 4x - 15$

37. $6x^2 - 19x + 15$

38. $2x^2 - x - 15$

39. $3x^2 - 7x - 6$

40. $2x^2 - 5x - 12$

41. $6x^2 - 7x - 5$

42. $4x^2 + 7x + 3$

43. $12y^2 - 7y + 1$

44. $6y^2 - 5y + 1$

45. $6x^2 - 11x + 4$

46. $12x^2 + 19x + 5$

47. $7y^2 + 47y - 14$

48. $11x^2 - 54x - 5$

49. $15x^2 - 19x + 6$

50. $8x^2 - 30x + 25$

51. $14y^2 + 15y - 9$

52. $22x^2 + 51x - 10$

53. $14x^2 - 41x + 15$

54. $8y^2 + 17y + 9$

55. $8x^2 + 65x + 8$

56. $20x^2 + 37x + 15$

57. $24y^2 + 41y + 12$

58. $18x^2 - 27x + 4$

59. $10x^2 + 3x - 4$

60. $10y^2 - 29y + 10$

Practice 9-7

Factor each expression.

1. $x^2 - 9$

2. $4m^2 - 1$

3. $a^2 + 2a + 1$

4. $4x^2 + 12x + 9$

5. $x^2 - 22x + 121$

6. $n^2 - 4$

7. $9x^2 - 4$

8. $16c^2 - 49$

9. $9x^2 - 30x + 25$

10. $4x^2 - 20x + 25$

11. $2a^2 - 18$

12. $x^2 - 24x + 144$

13. $3n^2 - 3$

14. $9h^2 + 60h + 100$

15. $9d^2 - 49$

16. $81a^2 - 400$

17. $r^2 - 36$

18. $3a^2 - 48$

19. $b^2 + 4b + 4$

20. $10x^2 - 90$

21. $25x^2 - 64$

22. $12w^2 - 27$

23. $g^3 - 25g$

24. $x^2 + 6x + 9$

25. $a^2 - 25$

26. $36s^2 - 225$

27. $4b^2 + 44b + 121$

28. $x^2 - 16x + 64$

29. $x^2 - 2x + 1$

30. $d^2 - 49$

31. $x^3 - 36x$

32. $9y^2 - 289$

33. $x^2 - 30x + 225$

34. $100a^2 - 9$

35. $2x^2 + 4x + 2$

36. $5n^3 - 20n$

37. $9n^2 + 12n + 4$

38. $d^2 - 169$

39. $4a^2 - 81$

40. $x^2 - 121$

41. $5x^2 + 40x + 80$

42. $16n^2 + 56n + 49$

43. $3n^2 - 30n + 75$

44. $a^2 + 26a + 169$

45. $25x^2 - 144$

46. $9d^2 - 64$

47. $n^2 - 28n + 196$

48. $49a^2 - 14a + 1$

49. $y^2 + 8y + 16$

50. $y^2 - 400$

51. $x^2 - 10x + 25$

52. $4x^2 - 60x + 225$

53. $3x^2 - 363$

54. $y^2 - 81$

55. $a^2 - 100$

56. $256a^2 - 1$

57. $n^2 + 34n + 289$

58. $2d^3 - 50d$

59. $y^2 + 22y + 121$

60. $144x^2 - 25$

61. $4x^2 - 169$

62. $x^2 - 12x + 36$

63. $64r^2 + 80r + 25$

64. $50m^3 - 32m$

65. $b^2 - 225$

66. $x^2 - 18x + 81$

67. $b^2 - 64$

68. $16x^2 - 72x + 81$

69. $b^2 - 256$

70. $x^2 + 24x + 144$

71. $225x^2 - 16$

72. $2x^3 + 40x^2 + 200x$

73. $4r^2 - 25$

74. $16x^2 + 8x + 1$

75. $b^2 - 14b + 49$

76. $x^2 + 30x + 225$

77. $m^2 - 28m + 196$

78. $9r^2 - 256$

79. $b^2 + 20b + 100$

80. $m^2 - 16$

81. $4x^2 - 32x + 64$

82. $x^2 - 196$

83. $8x^3 - 32x$

84. $25x^2 - 30x + 9$

85. $8m^2 - 16m + 8$

86. $9x^2 - 400$

87. $m^2 - 144$

Practice 9-8

Factor each expression.

1. $x(a + 2) - 2(a + 2)$

2. $3(x + y) + a(x + y)$

3. $m(x - 3) + k(x - 3)$

4. $a(y + 1) - b(y + 1)$

5. $x^2 + 3x + 2xy + 6y$

6. $y^2 - 5wy + 4y - 20w$

7. $xy + 4y - 2x - 8$

8. $ab + 7b - 3a - 21$

9. $ax + bx + ay + by$

10. $ax + bx - ay - by$

11. $2x^2 - 6xy + 5x - 15y$

12. $3x^2 - 6xy + 2x - 4y$

13. $2ax + 6xc + ba + 3bc$

14. $x^2y - 3x^2 - 2y + 6$

15. $6 + 2y + 3x^2 + x^2y$

16. $2x^2 - 3x + 1$

17. $2x^2 - 7x + 3$

18. $6x^2 + 7x + 2$

19. $4x^2 + 8x + 3$

20. $6x^2 - 7x + 2$

21. $4x^2 - 9x + 2$

22. $2x^2 - 3x - 2$

23. $12x^2 - x - 1$

24. $6x^2 + 19x + 3$

25. $12y^2 - 5y - 2$

26. $10y^2 + 21y - 10$

27. $5y^2 + 13y + 6$

28. $16y^2 + 10y + 1$

29. $16x^2 - 14x + 3$

30. $16x^2 + 16x + 3$

31. $10x^2 - 3x - 1$

32. $9x^2 + 25x - 6$

33. $14x^2 + 15x - 9$

34. $2x^3 + 8x^2 + x + 4$

35. $8x^4 + 6x - 28x^3 - 21$

36. $5x^3 - x^2 + 15x - 3$

37. $x^3 + 3x^2 + 4x + 12$

38. $6x^3 + 3x^2 + 2x + 1$

39. $3x^3 + 9x^2 + 2x + 6$

40. $9x^3 - 12x^2 + 3x - 4$

41. $10x^3 - 25x^2 + 4x - 10$

42. $4x^3 - 20x^2 + 3x - 15$

Find expressions for the possible dimensions of each rectangular prism.

43. The volume of the prism is given.

44. The volume of the prism is given.

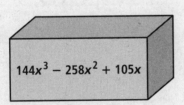

$144x^3 - 258x^2 + 105x$

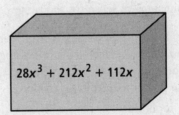

$28x^3 + 212x^2 + 112x$

Practice 10-1

Identify the vertex of each graph. Tell whether it is a minimum or a maximum.

1. $y = -3x^2$

2. $y = -7x^2$

3. $y = 0.5x^2$

4. $y = 5x^2$

5. $y = -4x^2$

6. $y = \frac{3}{2}x^2$

Order each group of quadratic functions from widest to narrowest graph.

7. $y = x^2, y = 5x^2, y = 3x^2$

8. $y = -8x^2, y = \frac{1}{2}x^2, y = -x^2$

9. $y = 5x^2, y = -4x^2, y = 2x^2$

10. $y = -\frac{1}{2}x^2, y = \frac{1}{3}x^2, y = -3x^2$

11. $y = 6x^2, y = -7x^2, y = 4x^2$

12. $y = \frac{3}{4}x^2, y = 2x^2, y = \frac{1}{5}x^2$

Graph each function.

13. $y = x^2$

14. $y = 4x^2$

15. $y = -3x^2$

16. $y = -x^2 - 4$

17. $y = 2x^2 - 2$

18. $y = 2x^2 + 3$

19. $y = \frac{1}{2}x^2 + 2$

20. $y = \frac{1}{2}x^2 - 3$

21. $y = \frac{1}{3}x^2 + 5$

22. $y = \frac{1}{3}x^2 - 4$

23. $y = 2.5x^2 + 3$

24. $y = 2.5x^2 + 5$

25. $y = 5x^2 + 8$

26. $y = 5x^2 - 8$

27. $y = -3.5x^2 - 4$

28. The price of a stock on the NYSE is modeled by the function $y = 0.005x^2 + 10$, where x is the number of months the stock has been available.

   a. Graph the function.

   b. What x-values make sense for the domain? Explain why.

   c. What y-values make sense for the range? Explain why.

29. You are designing a poster. The poster is 24 in. wide by 36 in. high. On the poster, you want to place a square photograph and some printing. If each side of the photograph is x in., the function $y = 864 - x^2$ gives the area of the poster available for printing.

   a. Graph the function.

   b. What x-values make sense for the domain? Explain why.

   c. What y-values make sense for the range? Explain why.

30. You are placing a circular drawing on a square piece of poster board. The poster board is 15 in. wide. The part of the poster board not covered by the drawing will be painted blue. If the radius of the drawing is r, the function $A = 225 - 3.14r^2$ gives the area to be painted blue.

   a. Graph the function.

   b. What x-values make sense for the domain? Explain why.

   c. What y-values make sense for the range? Explain why.

Practice 10-2

Find the equation of the axis of symmetry and the coordinates of the vertex of the graph of each function.

1. $y = x^2 - 10x + 2$

2. $y = x^2 + 12x - 9$

3. $y = -x^2 + 2x + 1$

4. $y = 3x^2 + 18x + 9$

5. $y = 3x^2 + 3$

6. $y = 16x - 4x^2$

7. $y = 0.5x^2 + 4x - 2$

8. $y = -4x^2 + 24x + 6$

9. $y = -1.5x^2 + 6x$

Graph each function. Label the axis of symmetry, the vertex, and the y-intercept.

10. $y = x^2 - 6x + 4$

11. $y = x^2 + 4x - 1$

12. $y = x^2 + 10x + 14$

13. $y = x^2 + 2x + 1$

14. $y = -x^2 - 4x + 4$

15. $y = -4x^2 + 24x + 13$

16. $y = -2x^2 - 8x + 5$

17. $y = 4x^2 - 16x + 10$

18. $y = -x^2 + 6x + 5$

19. $y = 4x^2 + 8x$

20. $y = -3x^2 + 6$

21. $y = 6x^2 + 48x + 98$

Graph each quadratic inequality.

22. $y > x^2 + 1$

23. $y \geq x^2 - 4$

24. $y < -x^2 + 1$

25. $y > x^2 + 6x + 3$

26. $y < x^2 - 4x + 4$

27. $y < -x^2 + 2x - 3$

28. $y \geq -2x^2 - 8x - 5$

29. $y \leq -3x^2 + 6x + 1$

30. $y \geq 2x^2 - 4x - 3$

Find the vertex of each function. Determine whether the vertex is a maximum or minimum.

31. $y = 2x^2 - 12x + 9$

32. $y = -2x^2 - 16x - 33$

33. $y = -4x^2 + 4x - 1$

34. $y = -3.5x^2 - 14x - 10$

35. $y = 0.05x^2 - 3.2x + 4$

36. $y = -1.8x^2 + 16.2x - 18.2$

37. You and a friend are hiking in the mountains. You want to climb to a ledge that is 20 ft above you. The height of the grappling hook you throw is given by the function $h = -16t^2 - 32t + 5$. What is the maximum height of the grappling hook? Can you throw it high enough to reach the ledge?

38. The total profit made by an engineering firm is given by the function $p = x^2 - 25x + 5000$. Find the minimum profit made by the company.

39. You are trying to dunk a basketball. You need to jump 2.5 ft in the air to dunk the ball. The height that your feet are above the ground is given by the function $h = -16t^2 + 12t$. What is the maximum height your feet will be above the ground? Will you be able to dunk the basketball?

Practice 10-3

Tell whether each expression is *rational* or *irrational*.

1. $-\sqrt{64}$ **2.** $\sqrt{1600}$ **3.** $\pm\sqrt{160}$ **4.** $\sqrt{144}$

5. $\sqrt{125}$ **6.** $-\sqrt{340}$ **7.** $\sqrt{1.96}$ **8.** $-\sqrt{0.09}$

Use a calculator to find each square root to the nearest hundredth.

9. $\sqrt{20}$ **10.** $\sqrt{73}$ **11.** $-\sqrt{38}$ **12.** $\sqrt{130}$

13. $\sqrt{149.3}$ **14.** $-\sqrt{8.7}$ **15.** $\sqrt{213.8}$ **16.** $-\sqrt{320.7}$

17. $\sqrt{113.9}$ **18.** $-\sqrt{840.6}$ **19.** $-\sqrt{1348.9}$ **20.** $\sqrt{928.2}$

Simplify each expression.

21. $\sqrt{49}$ **22.** $-\sqrt{2.25}$ **23.** $\sqrt{\dfrac{1}{16}}$ **24.** $\sqrt{400}$

25. $\sqrt{6.25}$ **26.** $\pm\sqrt{\dfrac{36}{25}}$ **27.** $\sqrt{196}$ **28.** $\sqrt{2.56}$

29. $\sqrt{0.25}$ **30.** $\pm\sqrt{\dfrac{9}{100}}$ **31.** $\sqrt{576}$ **32.** $\pm\sqrt{\dfrac{121}{36}}$

33. $\sqrt{1600}$ **34.** $-\sqrt{0.04}$ **35.** $\sqrt{2500}$ **36.** $\sqrt{4.41}$

Between what two consecutive integers is each square root?

37. $\sqrt{40}$ **38.** $\sqrt{139}$ **39.** $-\sqrt{75}$ **40.** $\sqrt{93}$

41. $-\sqrt{105.6}$ **42.** $-\sqrt{173.2}$ **43.** $\sqrt{1123.7}$ **44.** $\sqrt{216.9}$

Solve the following problems. Round to the nearest tenth if necessary.

45. You are to put a metal brace inside a square shipping container. The formula $d = \sqrt{2x^2}$ gives the length of the metal brace, where x is the length of the side of the container. Find the length of the brace for each container side length.

     a. $x = 3$ ft   **b.** $x = 4.5$ ft   **c.** $x = 5$ ft   **d.** $x = 8$ ft

46. You are designing a cone-shaped storage container. Use the formula $r = \sqrt{\dfrac{3V}{\pi h}}$ to find the radius of the storage container. Find the radius when $V = 10,000$ ft^3 and $h = 10$ ft.

Practice 10-4

Solve each equation by finding square roots. If the equation has no real solution, write *no solution*. If the value is irrational, round to the nearest hundredth.

1. $x^2 = 16$ **2.** $x^2 - 144 = 0$ **3.** $3x^2 - 27 = 0$

4. $x^2 + 16 = 0$ **5.** $x^2 = 12$ **6.** $x^2 = 49$

7. $x^2 + 8 = -10$ **8.** $3x^2 = 300$ **9.** $2x^2 - 6 = 26$

10. $x^2 = 80$ **11.** $81x^2 - 10 = 15$ **12.** $2x^2 = 90$

13. $x^2 = 300$ **14.** $4x^2 + 9 = 41$ **15.** $2x^2 + 8 = 4$

16. $x^2 + 8 = 72$ **17.** $4x^2 + 6 = 7$ **18.** $x^2 = 121$

19. $5x^2 + 20 = 30$ **20.** $x^2 + 6 = 17$ **21.** $3x^2 + 1 = 54$

22. $2x^2 - 7 = 74$ **23.** $x^2 + 1 = 0$ **24.** $4x^2 - 8 = -20$

25. $9x^2 = 1$ **26.** $x^2 + 4 = 4$ **27.** $3x^2 = 1875$

28. $x^2 = 9$ **29.** $5x^2 - 980 = 0$ **30.** $x^2 - 10 = 100$

31. $4x^2 - 2 = 1$ **32.** $3x^2 - 75 = 0$ **33.** $x^2 + 25 = 0$

34. $2x^2 - 10 = -4$ **35.** $4x^2 + 3 = 3$ **36.** $4x^2 - 8 = 32$

37. $7x^2 + 8 = 15$ **38.** $x^2 + 1 = 26$ **39.** $6x^2 = -3$

40. $x^2 - 400 = 0$ **41.** $7x^2 - 8 = 20$ **42.** $2x^2 - 1400 = 0$

43. $5x^2 + 25 = 90$ **44.** $x^2 + 4x^2 = 20$ **45.** $5x^2 - 18 = -23$

46. $3x^2 - x^2 = 10$ **47.** $2x^2 + 6 - x^2 = 9$ **48.** $x^2 - 225 = 0$

49. $-3 + 4x^2 = 2$ **50.** $7x^2 - 1008 = 0$ **51.** $6x^2 - 6 = 12$

Solve each problem. If necessary, round to the nearest tenth.

52. You want to build a fence around a square garden that covers 506.25 ft^2. How many feet of fence will you need to complete the job?

53. The formula $A = 6s^2$ will calculate the surface area of a cube. Suppose you have a cube that has a surface area of 216 in.^{2}. What is the length of each side?

54. You drop a pencil out of a window that is 20 ft above the ground. Use the formula $V^2 = 64s$, where V is the speed and s is the distance fallen, to calculate the speed the pencil is traveling when it hits the ground.

55. Suppose you are going to construct a circular fish pond in your garden. You want the pond to cover an area of 300 ft^2. What is the radius of the pond?

56. During the construction of a skyscraper, a bolt fell from 400 ft. What was the speed of the bolt when it hit the ground? Use $V^2 = 64s$.

Practice 10-5

Factoring to Solve Quadratic Equations

Use the Zero-Product Property to solve each equation.

1. $(x + 5)(x - 3) = 0$

2. $(x - 2)(x + 9) = 0$

3. $(b - 12)(b + 12) = 0$

4. $(2n + 3)(n - 4) = 0$

5. $(x + 7)(4x - 5) = 0$

6. $(2x + 7)(2x - 7) = 0$

7. $(3x - 7)(2x + 1) = 0$

8. $(8y - 3)(4y + 1) = 0$

9. $(5x + 6)(4x + 5) = 0$

Solve by factoring.

10. $x^2 + 5x + 6 = 0$

11. $b^2 - 7b - 18 = 0$

12. $r^2 - 4 = 0$

13. $x^2 + 8x - 20 = 0$

14. $y^2 + 14y + 13 = 0$

15. $s^2 - 3s - 10 = 0$

16. $x^2 + 7x = 8$

17. $x^2 = 25$

18. $h^2 + 10h = -21$

19. $2t^2 + 8t - 64 = 0$

20. $3a^2 - 36a + 81 = 0$

21. $5x^2 - 45 = 0$

22. $2a^2 - a - 21 = 0$

23. $3n^2 - 11n + 10 = 0$

24. $2x^2 - 7x - 9 = 0$

25. $2n^2 - 5n = 12$

26. $3m^2 - 5m = -2$

27. $5s^2 - 17s = -6$

28. $6m^2 = 13m + 28$

29. $4a^2 - 4a = 15$

30. $4r^2 = r + 3$

31. Suppose you are building a storage box of volume 4368 in.³. The length of the box will be 24 in. The height of the box will be 1 in. more than its width. Find the height and width of the box.

32. A banner is in the shape of a right triangle of area 63 in.². The height of the banner is 4 in. less than twice the width of the banner. Find the height and width of the banner.

33. A rectangular poster has an area of 190 in.². The height of the poster is 1 in. less than twice its width. Find the dimensions of the poster.

34. A diver is standing on a platform 24 ft above the pool. He jumps from the platform with an initial upward velocity of 8 ft/s. Use the formula $h = -16t^2 + vt + s$, where h is his height above the water, t is the time, v is his starting upward velocity, and s is his starting height. How long will it take for him to hit the water?

Solve each equation.

35. $(x - 9)(x + 8) = 0$

36. $x^2 - 9x - 10 = 0$

37. $(c - 21)(c + 21) = 0$

38. $(x - 12)(5x - 13) = 0$

39. $2a^2 - 21a - 65 = 0$

40. $x^2 + 6x - 91 = 0$

41. $a^2 + 6a - 72 = 0$

42. $4x^2 + 8x - 21 = 0$

43. $20d^2 - 82d + 80 = 0$

44. $3n^2 + 12n - 288 = 0$

45. $2s^2 - 13s - 24 = 0$

46. $x^2 + 5x = 150$

47. $3c^2 + 8c = 3$

48. $30a^2 + 121a - 21 = 0$

49. $c^2 - 81 = 0$

50. $x^2 + 306 = -35x$

51. $x^2 = 121$

52. $x^2 - 21x + 108 = 0$

Practice 10-6

Find the value of c such that each expression is a perfect square trinomial.

1. $x^2 - 14x + c$

2. $x^2 - \frac{2}{9}x + c$

3. $x^2 - \frac{4}{9}x + c$

4. $x^2 - \frac{2}{6}x + c$

Solve each equation by completing the square.

5. $x^2 - 4x = 5$

6. $x^2 - x - 2 = 0$

7. $x^2 - 6x = 10$

8. $x^2 + 4x + 4 = 0$

9. $x^2 - 3x = 18$

10. $x^2 - 8x - 4 = 0$

11. $x^2 - 6x = 0$

12. $x^2 - 6x = 8$

13. $x^2 - 7x = 0$

14. $x^2 + 4x - 12 = 0$

15. $x^2 + 11x + 10 = 0$

16. $x^2 + 2x = 15$

17. $x^2 - 8x = 9$

18. $x^2 + 5x = -6$

19. $x^2 - 2x = 120$

20. $x^2 - 22x = -105$

21. $2x^2 = 3x + 9$

22. $2x^2 + 8x - 10 = 0$

23. $2x^2 - 3x - 2 = 0$

24. $2x^2 + 12x - 32 = 0$

25. $3x^2 + 17x - 6 = 0$

26. $2x^2 - x - 28 = 0$

27. $3x^2 - 4x + 1 = 0$

28. $2x^2 - 5x - 3 = 0$

29. $6x^2 - 2x = 28$

30. $2x^2 - 16x = -30$

31. $4x^2 = -2x + 12$

32. $9x^2 + 6x = 3$

33. $10x^2 + 3x = 4$

34. $12x^2 - 29x + 15 = 0$

Practice 10-7

Use the quadratic formula to solve each equation. If the equation has no real solutions write *no real solutions.* If necessary, round your answers to the nearest hundredth.

1. $x^2 + 8x + 5 = 0$ **2.** $x^2 - 36 = 0$ **3.** $d^2 - 4d - 96 = 0$

4. $a^2 - 3a - 154 = 0$ **5.** $4p^2 - 12p - 91 = 0$ **6.** $5m^2 + 9m = 126$

7. $r^2 - 35r + 70 = 0$ **8.** $y^2 + 6y - 247 = 0$ **9.** $x^2 + 12x - 40 = 0$

10. $4n^2 - 81 = 0$ **11.** $x^2 + 13x + 30 = 0$ **12.** $a^2 - a = 132$

13. $6w^2 - 23w + 7 = 0$ **14.** $4x^2 + 33x = 27$ **15.** $7s^2 - 7 = 0$

16. $x^2 + 5x - 90 = 0$ **17.** $5b^2 - 20 = 0$ **18.** $4x^2 - 3x + 6 = 0$

19. $6h^2 + 77h - 13 = 0$ **20.** $5y^2 = 17y + 12$ **21.** $g^2 - 15g = 54$

22. $27f^2 = 12$ **23.** $4x^2 - 52x + 133 = 0$ **24.** $x^2 + 36x + 60 = 0$

25. $a^2 - 2a - 360 = 0$ **26.** $x^2 + 10x + 40 = 0$ **27.** $t^2 - 10t = 39$

28. $4x^2 + 7x - 9 = 0$ **29.** $2c^2 - 39c + 135 = 0$ **30.** $4x^2 + 33x + 340 = 0$

31. $m^2 - 40m + 100 = 0$ **32.** $8x^2 + 25x + 19 = 0$ **33.** $36w^2 - 289 = 0$

34. $4d^2 + 29d - 60 = 0$ **35.** $4z^2 + 43z + 108 = 0$ **36.** $3x^2 - 19x + 40 = 0$

37. $14x^2 = 56$ **38.** $32x^2 - 18 = 0$ **39.** $r^2 + r - 650 = 0$

40. $2y^2 = 39y - 17$ **41.** $5a^2 - 9a + 5 = 0$ **42.** $x^2 = 9x + 120$

43. $8h^2 - 38h + 9 = 0$ **44.** $20x^2 = 245$ **45.** $9h^2 - 72h = -119$

46. $x^2 + 3x + 8 = 0$ **47.** $6m^2 - 13m = 19$ **48.** $9x^2 - 81 = 0$

49. $4s^2 + 8s = 221$ **50.** $6p^2 + 25p - 119 = 0$ **51.** $2s^2 - 59s + 17 = 0$

52. A rectangular painting has dimensions x and $x + 10$. The painting is in a frame 2 in. wide. The total area of the picture and the frame is 900 in.^{2}. What are the dimensions of the painting?

53. A ball is thrown upward from a height of 15 ft with an inital upward velocity of 5 ft/s. Use the formula $h = -16t^2 + vt + s$ to find how long it will take for the ball to hit the ground.

54. Your community wants to put a square fountain in a park. Around the fountain will be a sidewalk that is 3.5 ft wide. The total area that the fountain and sidewalk can be is 700 ft^2. What are the dimensions of the fountain?

55. The Garys have a triangular pennant of area 420 in.^{2} flying from the flagpole in their yard. The height of the triangle is 10 in. less than 5 times the base of the triangle. What are the dimensions of the pennant?

Practice 10-8

Find the number of real solutions of each equation.

1. $x^2 + 6x + 10 = 0$ **2.** $x^2 - 4x - 1 = 0$ **3.** $x^2 + 6x + 9 = 0$

4. $x^2 - 8x + 15 = 0$ **5.** $x^2 - 5x + 7 = 0$ **6.** $x^2 - 4x + 5 = 0$

7. $3x^2 - 18x + 27 = 0$ **8.** $4x^2 - 8 = 0$ **9.** $-5x^2 - 10x = 0$

10. $-x^2 = 4x + 6$ **11.** $4x^2 = 9x - 3$ **12.** $8x^2 + 2 = 8x$

13. $7x^2 + 16x + 11 = 0$ **14.** $12x^2 - 11x - 2 = 0$ **15.** $-9x^2 - 25x + 20 = 0$

16. $16x^2 + 8x = -1$ **17.** $-16x^2 + 11x = 11$ **18.** $12x^2 - 12x = -3$

19. $0.2x^2 + 4.5x - 2.8 = 0$ **20.** $-2.8x^2 + 3.1x = -0.5$ **21.** $0.5x^2 + 0.6x = 0$

22. $1.5x^2 - 15x + 2.5 = 0$ **23.** $-3x^2 + 27x = -40$ **24.** $2.1x^2 + 4.2 = 0$

25. One of the games at a carnival involves trying to ring a bell with a ball by hitting a lever that propels the ball into the air. The height of the ball is modeled by the equation $h = -16t^2 + 39t$. If the bell is 25 ft above the ground, will it be hit by the ball?

26. You are placing a rectangular picture on a square poster board. You can enlarge the picture to any size. The area of the poster board not covered by the picture is modeled by the equation $A = -x^2 - 10x + 300$. Is it possible for the area not covered by the picture to be 100 in.^{2}?

27. The equation $h = -16t^2 + 58t + 3$ models the height of a baseball t seconds after it has been hit.

  a. Was the height of the baseball ever 40 ft?

  b. Was the height of the baseball ever 60 ft?

28. A firefighter is on the fifth floor of an office building. She needs to throw a rope into the window above her on the seventh floor. The function $h = -16t^2 + 36t$ models how high above her she is able to throw a rope. If she needs to throw the rope 40 ft above her to reach the seventh-floor window, will the rope get to the window?

Find the number of x-intercepts of each function.

29. $y = x^2 + 10x + 16$ **30.** $y = x^2 + 3x + 5$ **31.** $y = x^2 - 2x - 7$

32. $y = 3x^2 - 3$ **33.** $y = 2x^2 + x$ **34.** $y = 3x^2 + 2x + 1$

35. $y = x^2 - 8x - 4$ **36.** $y = x^2 - 16x + 64$ **37.** $y = -2x^2 - 5x - 6$

38. $y = -4x^2 - 5x - 2$ **39.** $y = -x^2 + 12x - 36$ **40.** $y = -5x^2 + 11x - 6$

Practice 10-9

Choosing a Linear, Quadratic, or Exponential Model

Which kind of function best models the data? Write an equation to model the data.

1. $(-1, 3), (1, 3), (3, 27), (5, 75), (7, 147)$

2. $(-2, 4), (-1, 2), (0, 0), (1, -2), (2, -4)$

3. $\left(-2, \frac{1}{16}\right), \left(-1, \frac{1}{4}\right), (0, 1), (1, 4), (2, 16)$

4. $(-6, -1), (-3, 0), (0, 1), (3, 2), (6, 3)$

5. $\left(-2, \frac{1}{3}\right), (-1, 1), (0, 3), (1, 9), (2, 27)$

6. $(-4, -32), (-2, -8), (0, 0), (2, -8), (4, -32)$

7.

x	y
-3	$\frac{9}{2}$
-2	2
-1	$\frac{1}{2}$
0	0

8.

x	y
-1	-2
0	-4
1	-6
2	-8

9.

x	y
-4	-4
-2	-1
0	0
2	-1

10.

x	y
0	-2
1	-8
2	-32
3	-128

11.

x	y
-7	-245
-5	-125
-3	-45
-1	-5

12.

x	y
-2	$\frac{3}{2}$
0	$\frac{1}{2}$
2	$-\frac{1}{2}$
4	$-\frac{3}{2}$

13. $\left(-2, \frac{1}{3}\right), \left(-1, \frac{1}{3}\right), \left(0, \frac{1}{3}\right), \left(1, \frac{1}{3}\right), \left(2, \frac{1}{3}\right)$

14. $\left(-1, -\frac{1}{4}\right), \left(0, -\frac{1}{2}\right), (1, -1), (2, -2), (3, -4)$

15. The cost of shipping computers from a warehouse is given in the table below.

Number of Computers	50	75	100	125
Cost (dollars)	1700	2500	3300	4100

   a. Determine which kind of function best models the data.

   b. Write an equation to model the data.

   c. On the basis of your equation, what is the cost of shipping 27 computers?

   d. On the basis of your equation, how many computers could be shipped for $5500?

16. During a scientific experiment, the bacteria count was taken at 5-min intervals. The data shows the count at several time periods during the experiment.

Time Interval	0	1	2	3
Count	110	132	159	190

   a. Determine which kind of function best models the data.

   b. Write an equation to model the data.

   c. On the basis of your equation, what is the count 1 hr, 45 min after the start of the experiment?

Practice 11-1

Simplify each radical expression. Assume that all variables under radicals represent positive numbers.

1. $\sqrt{32}$ **2.** $\sqrt{22} \cdot \sqrt{8}$ **3.** $\sqrt{147}$ **4.** $\sqrt{\dfrac{17}{144}}$ **5.** $\sqrt{a^2 b^5}$

6. $\dfrac{2}{\sqrt{6}}$ **7.** $\sqrt{80}$ **8.** $\sqrt{27}$ **9.** $\dfrac{\sqrt{256}}{\sqrt{32}}$ **10.** $\dfrac{8}{\sqrt{7}}$

11. $\sqrt{12x^4}$ **12.** $\dfrac{\sqrt{96}}{\sqrt{12}}$ **13.** $\sqrt{200}$ **14.** $\sqrt{\dfrac{12}{225}}$ **15.** $\sqrt{15} \cdot \sqrt{6}$

16. $\sqrt{120}$ **17.** $\dfrac{4}{\sqrt{2a}}$ **18.** $\left(3\sqrt{2}\right)^3$ **19.** $\sqrt{250}$ **20.** $\dfrac{\sqrt{65}}{\sqrt{13}}$

21. $\sqrt{84}$ **22.** $\sqrt{\dfrac{18}{225}}$ **23.** $\sqrt{48s^3}$ **24.** $3\sqrt{24}$ **25.** $\sqrt{15} \cdot \sqrt{35}$

26. $\sqrt{160}$ **27.** $\dfrac{6}{\sqrt{3}}$ **28.** $\dfrac{\sqrt{48n^6}}{\sqrt{6n^3}}$ **29.** $\sqrt{136}$ **30.** $\sqrt{\dfrac{27x^2}{256}}$

31. $\sqrt{m^3 n^2}$ **32.** $\dfrac{\sqrt{180}}{\sqrt{9}}$ **33.** $\sqrt{18} \cdot \sqrt{8}$ **34.** $\left(10\sqrt{3}\right)^2$ **35.** $\sqrt{\dfrac{17}{64}}$

36. $\sqrt{50}$ **37.** $\sqrt{48}$ **38.** $\sqrt{20}$ **39.** $\sqrt{8}$ **40.** $\sqrt{25x^2}$

41. $\sqrt{\dfrac{7}{9}}$ **42.** $\sqrt{\dfrac{17}{64}}$ **43.** $\dfrac{\sqrt{48}}{\sqrt{8}}$ **44.** $\dfrac{\sqrt{120}}{\sqrt{10}}$ **45.** $\dfrac{5}{\sqrt{2}}$

46. $\sqrt{75}$ **47.** $\sqrt{300}$ **48.** $\sqrt{49a^3}$ **49.** $\sqrt{125}$ **50.** $\sqrt{28x^4}$

51. $\dfrac{7}{\sqrt{3}}$ **52.** $\sqrt{\dfrac{15}{49}}$ **53.** $\dfrac{\sqrt{60}}{\sqrt{12}}$ **54.** $\dfrac{3}{\sqrt{3}}$ **55.** $\dfrac{4}{\sqrt{8}}$

56. $\sqrt{72x^3}$ **57.** $\sqrt{50y^3}$ **58.** $\sqrt{45x^2 y^3}$ **59.** $\sqrt{\dfrac{44x^3}{9x}}$ **60.** $\dfrac{\sqrt{4}}{\sqrt{3x}}$

61. $6\sqrt{20}$ **62.** $\sqrt{ab^3}$ **63.** $\sqrt{a^5 b^6}$ **64.** $12\sqrt{60x^2}$ **65.** $\left(2\sqrt{3}\right)^2$

66. $\sqrt{12} \cdot \sqrt{27}$ **67.** $\left(7\sqrt{5}\right)^2$ **68.** $\sqrt{14} \cdot \sqrt{8}$ **69.** $\left(5\sqrt{5}\right)^2$ **70.** $\sqrt{8x^6 y^7}$

71. $\sqrt{16a^3} \cdot \sqrt{5a^2}$ **72.** $\sqrt{8} \cdot \sqrt{7}$ **73.** $\sqrt{3x} \cdot \sqrt{5x}$ **74.** $2\sqrt{5} \cdot 2\sqrt{5}$

75. $4\sqrt{3} \cdot 2\sqrt{2}$ **76.** $6\sqrt{3} \cdot 7\sqrt{8}$ **77.** $\dfrac{10}{\sqrt{x}}$ **78.** $\dfrac{\sqrt{9}}{\sqrt{2x}}$

79. $\dfrac{4}{\sqrt{20}}$ **80.** $\dfrac{\sqrt{12x}}{\sqrt{27x}}$ **81.** $\dfrac{3\sqrt{7}}{\sqrt{20x}}$ **82.** $\dfrac{4\sqrt{5}}{\sqrt{8y}}$

Practice 11-2

The Pythagorean Theorem

• •

**Use the triangle at the right.
Find the length of the missing
side to the nearest tenth.**

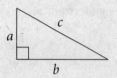

1. $a = 12, b = 35, c = $ ▇ 2. $a = 10, b = $ ▇$, c = 26$ 3. $a = 11, b = $ ▇$, c = 61$

4. $a = 36, b = 15, c = $ ▇ 5. $a = 8, b = 15, c = $ ▇ 6. $a = $ ▇$, b = 24, c = 40$

7. $a = 18, b = $ ▇$, c = 35$ 8. $a = 17, b = $ ▇$, c = 49$ 9. $a = 42, b = 37, c = $ ▇

10. $a = $ ▇$, b = 80, c = 90$ 11. $a = 8, b = 8, c = $ ▇ 12. $a = 19, b = $ ▇$, c = 26$

13. $a = $ ▇$, b = 27, c = 33$ 14. $a = $ ▇$, b = 13, c = 24$ 15. $a = 9, b = $ ▇$, c = 13$

16. $a = 19, b = 45, c = $ ▇ 17. $a = $ ▇$, b = 24, c = 39$ 18. $a = 14, b = 14, c = $ ▇

Determine whether the given lengths are sides of a right triangle.

19. $20, 21, 29$ 20. $16, 30, 34$ 21. $24, 60, 66$ 22. $23, 18, 14$

23. $10, 24, 28$ 24. $45, 28, 53$ 25. $\frac{4}{5}, \frac{3}{5}, 1$ 26. $\frac{2}{3}, \frac{4}{3}, \frac{1}{3}$

27. $3.5, 4.4, 5.5$ 28. $10.5, 11.3, 13.8$ 29. $3.3, 6.5, 5.6$ 30. $24, 70, 74$

31. $4.2, 7.0, 5.6$ 32. $5.2, 6.5, 3.9$ 33. $2.1, 3.5, 2.8$ 34. $4.8, 7.5, 5.4$

35. $7.5, 4.3, 6.7$ 36. $\frac{1}{9}, \frac{1}{15}, \frac{1}{18}$ 37. $\frac{1}{2}, \frac{6}{5}, \frac{13}{10}$ 38. $\frac{1}{5}, \frac{1}{4}, \frac{1}{3}$

Find the missing length to the nearest tenth.

39. A ladder is 25 ft long. The ladder needs to reach to a window that is
    24 ft above the ground. How far away from the building should the
    bottom of the ladder be placed?

40. Suppose you are making a sail in the shape of a right triangle for a
    sailboat. The length of the longest side of the sail is 65 ft. The sail is to
    be 63 ft high. What is the length of the third side of the sail?

41. Suppose you leave your house and travel 13 mi due west. Then you
    travel 3 mi due south. How far are you from your house?

42. A wire is run between the tips of two poles. One pole is 23 ft taller than
    the other pole. The poles are 37 ft apart. How long does the wire need
    to be to reach between the two poles?

43. A 20-ft-long wire is used to support a television antenna. The wire is
    connected to the antenna 15 ft above the ground. How far away from
    the base of the tower will the other end of the wire be located?

Practice 11-3

The Distance and Midpoint Formulas

Find the midpoint of $\overline{XY}$.

1. $X(8, 14)$ and $Y(2, 6)$

2. $X(11, 7)$ and $Y(3, 19)$

3. $X(-7, 6)$ and $Y(11, -2)$

4. $X(-3, -2)$ and $Y(7, 8)$

5. $X(-4, -1)$ and $Y(-8, 5)$

6. $X(6, 15)$ and $Y(4, 8)$

7. $X(-3, 5)$ and $Y(8, 9)$

8. $X(16, -8)$ and $Y(5, 9)$

9. $X(0, -15)$ and $Y(9, -15)$

10. $X(9\frac{1}{2}, 7)$ and $Y(7\frac{1}{2}, 5)$

11. $X(6, -2)$ and $Y(9, -1)$

12. $X(8, -13)$ and $Y(1, -7)$

13. $X(-7, -5)$ and $Y(-3, 16)$

14. $X(-7, -17)$ and $Y(11, 4)$

15. $X(11, 19)$ and $Y(6, -4)$

16. $X(3, -8)$ and $Y(-5, -13)$

17. $X(-2, 2)$ and $Y(6, -13)$

18. $X(-9, -4)$ and $Y(16, 12)$

Find the distance between each pair of points. If necessary, round to the nearest tenth.

19. $(3, 0), (0, 4)$

20. $(3, 5), (12, 17)$

21. $(-4, 2), (2, -6)$

22. $(5, -7), (9, -2)$

23. $(4, 9), (15, 4)$

24. $(-7, 4), (2, -9)$

25. $(6, -1), (-5, 5)$

26. $(9, 8), (1, 12)$

27. $(13, -8), (2, 15)$

28. $(16, -7), (-2, -3)$

29. $(9, 15), (5, 12)$

30. $(7, 5), (-9, -6)$

31. $(-7, 15), (19, 2)$

32. $(9, -1), (11, -28)$

33. $(14, -29), (10, -25)$

34. $(2, -8), (8, -1)$

35. $(-11, 1), (7, 13)$

36. $(-1, 9), (19, 23)$

37. $(-9, 33), (13, 31)$

38. $(7, 2), (1, -2)$

39. $\overline{AB}$ is a diameter of a circle. The coordinates of A are $(-1, 3)$, and the coordinates of B are $(-5, 9)$. Find the center of the circle.

40. $\overline{CD}$ is a diameter of a circle. The coordinates of C are $(-2, -3)$, and the coordinates of D are $(-12, -5)$. Find the center of the circle.

41. A quadrilateral is a parallelogram if the diagonals bisect each other. Quadrilateral $EFGH$ has vertices a $E(-4, 3)$, $F(2, 1)$, $G(4, 7)$, and $H(-2, 9)$. Find the midpoint of each diagonal. Is $EFGH$ a parallelogram? Explain.

42. A large building is on fire. Fire trucks from two different stations respond to the fire. One station is 1 mi east and 2 mi north of the fire. The other station is 2 mi west and 1 mi south of the fires. How far apart are the two fire stations?

43. The Anderson and McCready families decide to go to a concert together. The Andersons live 4 km west and 6 km north of the concert hall. The McCreadys live 5 km east and 2 km south of the concert hall. How far apart do the two families live?

44. According to the map, a ball field is 4 km west and 2 km north of where you live. A theater is 1 km east and 4 km south of where you live. How far apart are the ball field and the theater?

Practice 11-4

Operations with Radical Expressions

Simplify each expression.

1. $3\sqrt{7} + 5\sqrt{7}$

2. $10\sqrt{4} - \sqrt{4}$

3. $4\sqrt{2}\left(2 + 2\sqrt{3}\right)$

4. $\sqrt{45} + 2\sqrt{5}$

5. $12\sqrt{11} + 7\sqrt{11}$

6. $\sqrt{2}\left(2\sqrt{3} - 4\sqrt{2}\right)$

7. $\sqrt{28} + \sqrt{63}$

8. $3\sqrt{6} - 8\sqrt{6}$

9. $\sqrt{3}\left(\sqrt{6} - \sqrt{12}\right)$

10. $\sqrt{18} - \sqrt{50}$

11. $4\sqrt{2} + 2\sqrt{8}$

12. $13\sqrt{15} - 11\sqrt{15}$

13. $3\left(8\sqrt{3} - 7\right)$

14. $8\left(2\sqrt{5} + 5\sqrt{2}\right)$

15. $17\sqrt{21} - 12\sqrt{21}$

16. $\sqrt{6}\left(7 + 3\sqrt{3}\right)$

17. $8\left(4 - 3\sqrt{2}\right)$

18. $2\sqrt{12} + 6\sqrt{27}$

19. $19\sqrt{3} + \sqrt{12}$

20. $8\sqrt{26} + 10\sqrt{26}$

21. $\sqrt{10}\left(3 - 2\sqrt{6}\right)$

22. $9\sqrt{2} - \sqrt{50}$

23. $10\sqrt{13} - 7\sqrt{13}$

24. $12\sqrt{6} - 4\sqrt{24}$

25. $5\sqrt{7} + \sqrt{28}$

26. $8\sqrt{13} - 12\sqrt{13}$

27. $13\sqrt{40} + 6\sqrt{10}$

28. $-3\sqrt{3}\left(\sqrt{6} + \sqrt{3}\right)$

29. $12\sqrt{29} - 15\sqrt{29}$

30. $10\sqrt{6} - 2\sqrt{6}$

31. $8\sqrt{3} - \sqrt{75}$

32. $3\sqrt{6}\left(2\sqrt{3} + \sqrt{6}\right)$

33. $17\sqrt{35} + 2\sqrt{35}$

34. $\sqrt{19} + 4\sqrt{19}$

35. $12\sqrt{9} - 4\sqrt{9}$

36. $\sqrt{8}\left(\sqrt{2} - 7\right)$

37. $\dfrac{1}{\sqrt{2} - \sqrt{3}}$

38. $\dfrac{5}{\sqrt{7} - \sqrt{3}}$

39. $\dfrac{3}{\sqrt{5} + 5}$

40. $\left(\sqrt{6} - 3\right)^2$

41. $\left(3\sqrt{5} + \sqrt{5}\right)^2$

42. $\dfrac{7}{\sqrt{2} - \sqrt{7}}$

43. $\dfrac{3 - \sqrt{6}}{5 - 2\sqrt{6}}$

44. $\dfrac{-12}{\sqrt{6} - 3}$

45. $\dfrac{2\sqrt{3} - \sqrt{6}}{5\sqrt{3} + 2\sqrt{6}}$

Solve each exercise by using the golden ratio $\left(1 + \sqrt{5}\right) : 2$.

46. The ratio of the height : width of a window is equal to the golden ratio. The width of the door is 36 in. Find the height of the door. Express your answer in simplest radical form and in inches.

47. The ratio of the length : width of a flower garden is equal to the golden ratio. The width of the garden is 14 ft. Find the length of the garden. Express your answer is simplest radical form and in feet.

48. The ratio of the width : height of the front side of a building is equal to the golden ratio. The height of the building is 40 ft. Find the width of the building. Express your answer in simplest radical form and in feet.

Practice 11-5

Solve each radical equation. Check your solutions. If there is no solution, write *no solution*.

1. $\sqrt{x} + 3 = 11$

2. $\sqrt{x + 2} = \sqrt{3x - 6}$

3. $x = \sqrt{24 - 10x}$

4. $\sqrt{4x - 7} = 1$

5. $\sqrt{x} = \sqrt{4x - 12}$

6. $x = \sqrt{11x - 28}$

7. $\sqrt{x} = 12$

8. $x = \sqrt{12x - 32}$

9. $x = \sqrt{13x - 40}$

10. $\sqrt{3x + 5} = \sqrt{x + 1}$

11. $\sqrt{x + 3} = 5$

12. $\sqrt{6x - 4} = \sqrt{4x + 6}$

13. $2 = \sqrt{x + 6}$

14. $x = \sqrt{2 - x}$

15. $\sqrt{4x + 2} = \sqrt{x + 14}$

16. $\sqrt{x + 8} = 9$

17. $x = \sqrt{7x + 8}$

18. $\sqrt{3x + 8} = \sqrt{2x + 12}$

19. $\sqrt{2x + 3} = 5$

20. $\sqrt{3x + 13} = \sqrt{7x - 3}$

21. $x = \sqrt{6 + 5x}$

22. $\sqrt{3x - 5} = 4$

23. $\sqrt{3x + 4} = \sqrt{5x}$

24. $x = \sqrt{x - 12}$

25. $\sqrt{x - 4} + 3 = 9$

26. $x = \sqrt{8x + 20}$

27. $12 = \sqrt{6x}$

28. $x = \sqrt{60 - 7x}$

29. $\sqrt{x + 14} = \sqrt{6x - 1}$

30. $\sqrt{5x - 7} = \sqrt{6x + 11}$

31. $7 + \sqrt{2x} = 3$

32. $\sqrt{x + 56} = x$

33. $5 + \sqrt{x + 4} = 12$

34. The equation $d = \frac{1}{2}at^2$ gives the distance d in ft that an object travels from rest while accelerating, where a is the acceleration and t is the time.

   a. How far has an object traveled in 4 s when the acceleration is 5 ft/s²?

   b. How long does it take an object to travel 100 ft when the acceleration is 8 ft/s²?

35. The equation $v = 20\sqrt{t + 273}$ relates the speed v, in m/s, to the air temperature t in Celsius degrees.

   a. Find the temperature when the speed of sound is 340 m/s.

   b. Find the temperature when the speed of sound is 320 m/s.

36. The equation $V = \sqrt{\frac{Fr}{m}}$ gives the speed V in m/s of an object moving in a horizontal circle, where F is centripetal force, r is radius, and m is mass of the object.

   a. Find r when $F = 6$ N, $m = 2$ kg, and $V = 3$ m/s.

   b. Find F when $r = 1$ m, $m = 3$ kg, and $V = 2$ m/s.

Practice 11-6

Graphing Square Root Functions

Find the domain of each function.

1. $f(x) = \sqrt{x - 7}$ **2.** $f(x) = \sqrt{3x - 12}$ **3.** $y = \sqrt{4x + 11}$

4. $y = \sqrt{x - 12}$ **5.** $f(x) = \sqrt{x + 14}$ **6.** $y = \sqrt{x + 8}$

7. $y = \sqrt{5x + 13}$ **8.** $y = \sqrt{2x}$ **9.** $y = \sqrt{6x}$

Use a table of values to graph each function.

10. $y = \sqrt{x} - 12$ **11.** $y = 3\sqrt{x}$ **12.** $y = \sqrt{x + 8}$

13. $y = \sqrt{x + 7} - 6$ **14.** $y = \sqrt{x - 6} - 8$ **15.** $y = \sqrt{x - 10}$

16. $y = 2\sqrt{x - 2}$ **17.** $y = \sqrt{x - 8} + 6$ **18.** $y = \sqrt{x} + 7$

Using expressions such as "shift up," "shift down," "shift left," and "shift right," describe how each of the graphs compare to the graph of $y = \sqrt{x}$.

19. $y = \sqrt{x} - 9$ **20.** $y = \sqrt{x} - 8$ **21.** $y = \sqrt{x + 20}$

22. $y = \sqrt{x - 19}$ **23.** $y = \sqrt{x + 18}$ **24.** $y = \sqrt{x - 32}$

25. $y = \sqrt{x} + 11$ **26.** $y = \sqrt{x + 14}$ **27.** $y = \sqrt{x - 4} - 7$

28. The number of people involved in recycling in a community is modeled by the function $n = 90\sqrt{3t} + 400$, where t is the number of months the recycling plant has been open.

   a. Graph the function.

   b. Find the number of people recycling when the plant has been open for 6 mo.

   c. Find the month when about 670 people were recycling.

29. The time t, in seconds, that it takes for an object to drop a distance d, in feet, is modeled by the function $t = \sqrt{\frac{d}{16}}$. Assume no air resistance.

   a. Graph the function.

   b. Find the time it takes for an object to fall 1000 ft.

   c. How far does an object fall in 10 s?

Practice 11-7

Use △ABC to evaluate each expression.

1. sin A 2. cos A 3. tan A

4. sin B 5. cos B 6. tan B

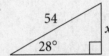

Evaluate each expression. Round to the nearest ten-thousandth.

7. tan 59°   8. sin 75°   9. sin 8°   10. cos 13°   11. sin 32°

12. tan 67°   13. cos 17°   14. cos 36°   15. tan 19°   16. cos 58°

Find the value of x to the nearest tenth.

17. 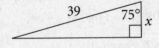   18. 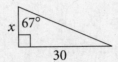   19.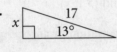

20. 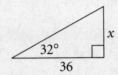   21. 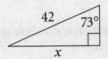   22.

Use △PQR to evaluate each expression.

23. sin P 24. cos P 25. tan P

26. sin R 27. cos R 28. tan R

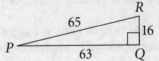

29. A tree casts a shadow that is 20 ft long. The angle of elevation of the sun is 29°. How tall is the tree?

30. Suppose your angle of elevation to the top of a water tower is 78°. If the water tower is 145 ft tall, how far are you standing from the water tower?

31. The angle of elevation from the control tower to an airplane is 49°. The airplane is flying at 5000 ft. How far away from the control tower is the plane?

32. A Boy Scout on top of a 1700-ft-tall mountain spots a campsite. If he measures the angle of depression at 35°, how far is the campsite from the foot of the mountain?

33. A 12-ft-long guy wire is attached to a telephone pole 10.5 ft from the top of the pole. If the wire forms a 52° angle with the ground, how high is the telephone pole?

Practice 12-1

Suppose y varies inversely with x. Write an equation for each inverse variation.

1. $x = 9$ when $y = 6$

2. $x = 3.6$ when $y = 5$

3. $x = \frac{3}{4}$ when $y = \frac{2}{9}$

4. $x = 7$ when $y = 13$

5. $x = 8$ when $y = 9$

6. $x = 4.9$ when $y = 0.8$

7. $x = 11$ when $y = 44$

8. $y = 8$ when $x = 9.5$

9. $y = 12$ when $x = \frac{5}{6}$

Each pair of points is on the graph of an inverse variation. Find the missing value.

10. $(5, 8)$ and $(4, m)$

11. $(16, 5)$ and $(10, h)$

12. $(14, 8)$ and $(c, 7)$

13. $(3, 18)$ and $(a, 27)$

14. $(4, 28)$ and $(3, p)$

15. $(100, 25)$ and $(4, a)$

16. $(x, 7)$ and $(2, 14)$

17. $\left(\frac{2}{5}, \frac{3}{2}\right)$ and $\left(k, \frac{5}{2}\right)$

18. $(16, 3)$ and $(g, 24)$

19. $(2.4, 19.8)$ and $(h, 13.2)$

20. $(12.4, 6.6)$ and $(f, 8.8)$

21. $(3.2, k)$ and $(9.2, 0.8)$

22. $(18, 24)$ and $(72, v)$

23. $(17, 0.9)$ and $(5.1, x)$

24. $\left(\frac{3}{4}, y\right)$ and $\left(\frac{2}{3}, 18\right)$

Explain whether each situation represents a direct variation or an inverse variation.

25. The cost of a $50 birthday gift is split among some friends.

26. You purchase some peaches at $1.29/lb.

Tell whether the data in each table is a *direct variation*, or an *inverse variation*. Write an equation to model the data.

27.

x	2	7	10
y	35	10	7

28.

x	3	6	24
y	16	8	2

29.

x	5	6	8
y	55	66	88

30.

x	2	8	16
y	9	36	72

31.

x	2	3	9
y	18	12	4

32

x	2	6	10
y	4.2	12.6	21

33.

x	2	5	12
y	12.8	32	76.8

34.

x	1.2	1.5	2.4
y	5	4	2.5

35.

x	6	9	36
y	3	2	0.5

36. The volume V of a gas in a closed container varies inversely with the pressure p, in atmospheres, that is applied to that gas.

   a. If $V = 20$ m^3 when $p = 1$ atm, find V when $p = 4$ atm.

   b. If $V = 24$ m^3 when $p = 3$ atm, find p when $V = 36$ m^3.

   c. If $V = 48$ m^3 when $p = 2$ atm, find V when $p = 5$ atm.

37. The time t to travel a fixed distance varies inversely with the rate r of travel.

   a. If $t = 3$ h and $r = 25$ mi/h, find t when $r = 50$ mi/h.

   b. If $t = 120$ s and $r = 40$ ft/s, find r when $t = 25$ s.

Practice 12-2

Describe the graph of each function.

1. $f(x) = x^2 - 4$ 　　　　**2.** $y = \frac{5}{x} - 1$ 　　　　**3.** $y = \frac{3}{x}$

4. $g(x) = \sqrt{x + 2} - 1$ 　　**5.** $y = -8x + 2$ 　　　**6.** $h(x) = 3x^2 - 4x + 1$

7. $h(x) = |2x + 7|$ 　　　　**8.** $y = 0.2^x$ 　　　　**9.** $y = \frac{x}{4}$

10. In an electric circuit the resistance R, in ohms, increases when the current I, in amps, in the circuit decreases. The function $R = \frac{1000}{I^2}$ relates the resistance to the current.

   a. What is the resistance when the current is 4 amps?

   b. What is the resistance when the current is 20 amps?

   c. What is the resistance when the current is 10 amps?

11. Light intensity decreases as you move farther away from the source of light. The function $I = \frac{12,000}{d^2}$ relates the light intensity I, in lumens, to the distance d, in feet, from the light source.

   a. What is the light intensity 2 ft away from the light source?

   b. What is the light intensity 8 ft away from the light source?

   c. What is the light intensity 25 ft away from the light source?

12. In a cylinder of constant volume, the height increases as the radius decreases. The function $h = \frac{360}{r^2}$ relates the height of the cylinder to the radius of the cylinder.

   a. What is the height of the cylinder when the radius is 5 m?

   b. What is the height of the cylinder when the radius is 12 m?

What value of x makes the denominator of each function equal to zero?

13. $y = \frac{5}{2x - 8}$ 　　**14.** $y = \frac{12}{x}$ 　　**15.** $y = \frac{5}{x + 7}$ 　　**16.** $y = \frac{5x}{4x - 10}$

17. $y = \frac{7x}{x + 3}$ 　　**18.** $y = \frac{3}{x - 8}$ 　　**19.** $y = \frac{6}{5x - 6}$ 　　**20.** $y = \frac{9x}{3x + 5}$

Graph each function. Include a dashed line for each asymptote.

21. $y = \frac{2}{x}$ 　　**22.** $y = \frac{2}{x - 1}$ 　　**23.** $y = \frac{1}{x + 4}$ 　　**24.** $y = \frac{2}{x} + 3$

25. $y = \frac{-2}{x + 6}$ 　　**26.** $y = \frac{2x}{x - 6}$ 　　**27.** $y = \frac{x + 3}{x - 2}$ 　　**28.** $y = \frac{3}{x - 1} - 3$

Practice 12-3

Simplify each expression.

1. $\dfrac{6x^4}{18x^2}$

2. $\dfrac{15a^2}{25a^4}$

3. $\dfrac{32h^3}{48h^2}$

4. $\dfrac{12n^4}{21n^6}$

5. $\dfrac{3x-6}{6}$

6. $\dfrac{x^2-2x}{x}$

7. $\dfrac{4t^2-2t}{2t}$

8. $\dfrac{a^3-2a^2}{2a^2-4a}$

9. $\dfrac{21x^2y}{14xy^2}$

10. $\dfrac{32x^3y^2}{24xy^4}$

11. $\dfrac{x^2+3x}{3x+9}$

12. $\dfrac{x^2-5x}{5x-25}$

13. $\dfrac{x^2+13x+12}{x^2-144}$

14. $\dfrac{x^2-9}{x^3-3x^2}$

15. $\dfrac{x^3+x^2}{x+1}$

16. $\dfrac{3x-2y}{2y-3x}$

17. $\dfrac{x^2+x-6}{x^2-x-2}$

18. $\dfrac{x^2+3x+2}{x^3+x^2}$

19. $\dfrac{2x^2-8}{x^2-3x+2}$

20. $\dfrac{2x^2-5x+3}{x^2-1}$

21. $\dfrac{3x+3y}{x^2+xy}$

22. $\dfrac{10+3x-x^2}{x^2-4x-5}$

23. $\dfrac{9-x^2}{x^2+x-12}$

24. $\dfrac{x^2+2x-15}{x^2-7x+12}$

25. $\dfrac{x^2+7x-8}{x^2+6x-7}$

26. $\dfrac{x^2+3x-10}{25-x^2}$

27. Write and simplify the ratio $\dfrac{\text{perimeter of rectangle}}{\text{area of rectangle}}$. The perimeter of
the rectangle is $10w$ and the area of the rectangle is $4w^2$.

28. The ratio $\dfrac{3 \cdot \text{volume of cone}}{\text{area of base}}$ determines the height of a cone. Find the
height when the volume is $4r^3 + 2r^2$ and the area of the base is $6r^2$.

29. The ratio $\dfrac{2 \cdot \text{area of triangle}}{\text{height of triangle}}$ determines the length of the base of a
triangle. Find the length of the base when the area is $3n^2 + 6n$ and the
height is $2n + 4$.

30. The ratio $\dfrac{\text{volume of rectangular solid}}{\text{area of rectangular base}}$ determines the height of a
rectangular solid. Find the height when the volume is $5s^3 + 10s^2$ and
the area is $5s^2$.

Practice 12-4

Multiplying and Dividing Rational Expressions

Find each product or quotient.

1. $\frac{5}{9} \cdot \frac{6}{15}$

2. $\frac{8}{3} \div \frac{16}{27}$

3. $\left(-\frac{3}{4}\right) \div \frac{16}{21}$

4. $\frac{2}{9} \div \left(-\frac{10}{3}\right)$

5. $\frac{18m}{4m^2} \div \frac{9m}{8}$

6. $\frac{8x}{12} \cdot \frac{4x}{6}$

7. $\frac{9}{15x} \cdot \frac{25x}{27}$

8. $\frac{12x^3}{25} \div \frac{16x}{5}$

9. $\frac{6x^3}{18x} \div \frac{9x^2}{10x^4}$

10. $\frac{4r^3}{10} \cdot \frac{25}{16r^2}$

11. $\frac{8n^2}{3} \div \frac{20n}{9}$

12. $\frac{14x^2}{5} \div 7x^4$

13. $\frac{4n^3}{11} \cdot \frac{33n}{36n^2}$

14. $\frac{24r^3}{35r^2} \div \frac{12r}{14r^3}$

15. $\frac{a^2 - 4}{3} \cdot \frac{9}{a + 2}$

16. $\frac{4b - 12}{5b^2} \cdot \frac{6b}{b - 3}$

17. $\frac{2b}{5} \cdot \frac{10}{b^2}$

18. $\frac{2b}{b + 3} \div \frac{b}{b + 3}$

19. $\frac{5y^3}{7} \cdot \frac{14y}{30y^2}$

20. $\frac{4p + 16}{5p} \div \frac{p + 4}{15p^3}$

21. $\frac{3(h + 2)}{h + 3} \div \frac{h + 2}{h + 3}$

22. $\frac{a^3 - a^2}{a^3} \cdot \frac{a^2}{a - 1}$

23. $\frac{h^2 + 6h}{h + 3} \cdot \frac{4h + 12}{h + 6}$

24. $\frac{n^2 - 1}{n + 2} \cdot \frac{n^2 - 4}{n + 1}$

25. $\frac{x^2 - x}{x} \cdot \frac{3x - 6}{3x - 3}$

26. $\frac{5x - 10}{x + 2} \cdot \frac{3}{3x - 6}$

27. $\frac{x^2 - 16}{x - 4} \div \frac{3x + 12}{x}$

28. $\frac{x^2 - 1}{3x - 3} \div \frac{x + 1}{3}$

29. $\frac{x^2 - 2x - 24}{x^2 - 5x - 6} \cdot \frac{x^2 + 5x + 6}{x^2 + 6x + 8}$

30. $\frac{x^2 + 2x - 35}{x^2 + 4x - 21} \cdot \frac{x^2 + 3x - 18}{x^2 + 9x + 18}$

31. $\frac{3x^2 + 14x + 8}{2x^2 + 7x - 4} \cdot \frac{2x^2 + 9x - 5}{3x^2 + 16x + 5}$

32. $\frac{8 + 2x - x^2}{x^2 + 7x + 10} \div \frac{x^2 - 11x + 28}{x^2 - x - 42}$

33. $\frac{x^2 - x - 6}{3x - 9} \cdot \frac{x^2 - 9}{x^2 + 6x + 9}$

34. $\frac{6x^2 + 13x + 6}{4x^2 - 9} \div \frac{6x^2 + x - 2}{4x^2 - 1}$

35. $\frac{x^2 - 2x - 35}{3x^2 + 27x} \div \frac{x^2 + 7x + 10}{6x^2 + 12x}$

36. $\frac{x^2 - x - 6}{2x^2 + 9x + 10} \div \frac{x^2 - 25}{2x^2 + 15x + 25}$

37. $\frac{15 - 14x - 8x^2}{4x^2 + 4x - 15} \div \frac{4x^2 + 13x - 12}{3x^2 + 13x + 4}$

38. $\frac{x^2 - 4x - 32}{x^2 - 8x - 48} \cdot \frac{3x^2 + 17x + 10}{3x^2 - 22x - 16}$

39. $\frac{9x^2 - 16}{6x^2 - 11x + 4} \div \frac{6x^2 + 11x + 4}{8x^2 + 10x + 3}$

40. Two darts are thrown at random onto the large rectangular region shown. Find the probability that both darts will land in the shaded region.

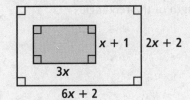

Practice 12-5

Divide.

1. $\dfrac{10x - 25}{5}$

2. $\dfrac{4x^3 - 3x}{x}$

3. $(3x^2 - 6x) \div 3x$

4. $(10x^2 - 6x) \div 2x$

5. $(-8x^5 + 16x^4 - 24x^3 + 32x^2) \div 8x^2$

6. $(15x^2 - 30x) \div 5x$

7. $(x^2 - 14x + 49) \div (x - 7)$

8. $(2x^2 - 13x + 21) \div (x - 3)$

9. $(4x^2 - 16) \div (2x + 4)$

10. $(x^2 + 4x - 12) \div (x - 2)$

11. $(x^2 + 10x + 16) \div (x + 2)$

12. $(12x^2 - 5x - 2) \div (3x - 2)$

13. $(x^2 + 5x + 10) \div (x + 2)$

14. $(x^2 - 8x - 9) \div (x - 3)$

15. $(3x^2 - 2x - 13) \div (x - 2)$

16. $(x^3 + 3x^2 + 5x + 3) \div (x + 1)$

17. $(5 - 23x + 12x^2) \div (4x - 1)$

18. $(24 + 6x^2 + 25x) \div (3x - 1)$

19. $(2x^2 + 11x - 5) \div (x + 6)$

20. $(x^2 + 5x - 10) \div (x + 2)$

21. $(8x + 3 + 4x^2) \div (2x - 1)$

22. $(3x^2 + 11x - 4) \div (3x - 1)$

23. $(x^3 + x - x^2 - 1) \div (x - 1)$

24. $(10 + 21x + 10x^2) \div (2x + 3)$

25. $(6x^2 - 35x + 36) \div (3x - 4)$

26. $(-2x^2 - 33x + x^3 - 7) \div (x - 7)$

27. The volume of a rectangular prism is $15x^3 + 38x^2 - 23x - 6$. The height of the prism is $5x + 1$, and the width of the prism is $x + 3$. Find the length of the prism.

28. The width of a rectangle is $x + 1$, and the area is $x^3 + 2x^2 - 5x - 6$ cm. What is the length of the rectangle?

Practice 12-6

Adding and Subtracting Rational Expressions

Simplify.

1. $\dfrac{3x}{4} - \dfrac{x}{4}$

2. $\dfrac{3}{x} + \dfrac{5}{x}$

3. $\dfrac{5x}{6} - \dfrac{2x}{3}$

4. $\dfrac{x}{3} + \dfrac{x}{5}$

5. $\dfrac{3m}{4} + \dfrac{5m}{12}$

6. $\dfrac{4x}{7} - \dfrac{3x}{14}$

7. $\dfrac{6}{7t} - \dfrac{3}{7t}$

8. $\dfrac{d}{3} + \dfrac{4d}{3}$

9. $\dfrac{7}{2d} - \dfrac{3}{2d}$

10. $\dfrac{3}{2d^2} + \dfrac{4}{3d}$

11. $\dfrac{9}{m+1} - \dfrac{6}{m-1}$

12. $\dfrac{3}{x} - \dfrac{7}{x}$

13. $\dfrac{7a}{6} + \dfrac{a}{6}$

14. $\dfrac{4}{k+3} - \dfrac{8}{k+3}$

15. $\dfrac{3}{4z^2} + \dfrac{7}{4z^2}$

16. $\dfrac{6}{x^2-1} + \dfrac{7}{x-1}$

17. $\dfrac{2x}{x^2-1} - \dfrac{3}{x+1}$

18. $\dfrac{3t}{8} + \dfrac{3t}{8}$

19. $\dfrac{4}{3a^2} - \dfrac{1}{2a^3}$

20. $\dfrac{4}{a+4} + \dfrac{6}{a+4}$

21. $\dfrac{4}{x+3} + \dfrac{6}{x-2}$

22. $\dfrac{6}{7t^3} - \dfrac{8}{3t}$

23. $\dfrac{3}{2x+6} + \dfrac{4}{6x+18}$

24. $\dfrac{5}{8a} - \dfrac{3}{8a}$

25. $\dfrac{5}{r^2-4} + \dfrac{7}{r+2}$

26. $\dfrac{6}{a^2-2} + \dfrac{9}{a^2-2}$

27. $\dfrac{5x}{4} - \dfrac{x}{4}$

28. $\dfrac{4}{3x+6} - \dfrac{3}{2x+4}$

29. $\dfrac{4}{c^2+4c+3} + \dfrac{1}{c+3}$

30. $\dfrac{6}{x^2-3x+2} - \dfrac{4}{x-2}$

31. Brian rode his bike 2 mi to his friend's house. Brian's bike had a flat tire, so he had to walk home. His walking rate is 25% of his biking rate.

   a. Write an expression for the amounts of time Brian spent walking and riding his bike.

   b. If Brian's biking rate is 12 mi/h, how much time did he spend walking and riding his bike?

32. Trudi and Sean are on a river canoeing. Because of the current of the river, their downstream rate is 250% of their upstream rate. They canoe 3 mi upstream and then return to their starting point.

   a. Write an expression for the amount of time Trudi and Sean spend canoeing.

   b. If their upstream rate is 2 mi/h, how much time do Trudi and Sean spend canoeing?

   c. If their upstream rate is 3 mi/h, how much time do Trudi and Sean spend canoeing?

Practice 12-7

Solving Rational Equations

Solve each equation. Check your solution.

1. $\frac{1}{x} + \frac{1}{2x} = \frac{1}{6}$

2. $\frac{x}{x+2} + \frac{4}{x-2} = 1$

3. $\frac{1}{3s} = \frac{s}{2} - \frac{1}{6s}$

4. $\frac{x+2}{x+8} = \frac{x-2}{x+4}$

5. $1 - \frac{3}{x} = \frac{4}{x^2}$

6. $\frac{7}{3(a-2)} - \frac{1}{a-2} = \frac{2}{3}$

7. $\frac{n}{n-4} = \frac{2n}{n+4}$

8. $x + \frac{6}{x} = -7$

9. $\frac{2}{r^2-r} - 1 = \frac{2}{r-1}$

10. $\frac{y}{y+3} = \frac{6}{y+9}$

11. $\frac{d}{3} + \frac{1}{2} = \frac{1}{3d}$

12. $\frac{2m}{m-5} = \frac{2m+16}{m+3}$

13. $\frac{1}{m-4} + \frac{1}{m+4} = \frac{8}{m^2-16}$

14. $\frac{5}{x-2} = \frac{5x+10}{x^2}$

15. $\frac{k^2}{k+3} = \frac{9}{k+3}$

16. $\frac{h-3}{h+6} = \frac{2h+3}{h+6}$

17. $\frac{h}{6} - \frac{3}{2h} = \frac{8}{3h}$

18. $4 - \frac{3}{y} = \frac{5}{y}$

19. $\frac{1}{b-3} = \frac{b}{4}$

20. $\frac{1}{t^2} - \frac{2}{t} = \frac{3}{t^2}$

21. $\frac{2}{3n} + \frac{3}{4} = \frac{2}{3}$

22. David and Fiona have a house painting business. It takes Fiona 3 days to paint a certain house. David could paint the same house in 4 days. How long would it take them to paint the house if David and Fiona worked together?

23. Suppose the Williams Spring Water Company has two machines that bottle the spring water. Machine X fills the bottles twice as fast as Machine Y. Working together, it takes them 20 min to fill 450 bottles. How long would it take each machine working alone to fill the 450 bottles?

24. Chao, who is an experienced architect, can draw a certain set of plans in 6 h. It takes Carl, who is a new architect, 10 h to draw the same set of plans. How long would it take them working together to draw the set of plans?

25. For exercise, Joseph likes to walk and Vincent likes to ride his bike. Vincent rides his bike 12 km/h faster than Joseph walks. Joseph walks 20 km in the same amount of time that Vincent rides 44 km. Find the rate that each of them travels.

26. The Ryan Publishing Company has two printing presses. It takes the new printing press 45 min to print 10,000 fliers. Together the two presses can print the 10,000 fliers in 30 min. How long does it take the older printing press by itself to print the 10,000 fliers?

Practice 12-8

Simplify each expression.

1. $_7P_2$ 2. $_{12}P_6$ 3. $_{11}P_3$ 4. $_{10}P_3$ 5. $_9P_8$ 6. $_{12}P_7$

7. $_{20}P_7$ 8. $_{15}P_3$ 9. $_{16}P_4$ 10. $_{25}P_3$ 11. $_{17}P_2$ 12. $_{15}P_2$

13. Suppose a license plate consists of five different letters.

   a. How many five-letter license plates are possible?

   b. In how many ways can a five-letter license plate be made with the letters from APRIL if none of the letters are repeated?

   c. Suppose a license plate is assigned randomly. What is the probability that it will contain the letters from APRIL?

14. In how many ways can nine mopeds be parked in a row?

15. Suppose there are three different ways in which you could go from your house to a friend's house. From your friend's house, there are four different ways in which you could go to the library. In how many different ways can you go from your house to the library after meeting your friend?

16. A sports card collection contains 20 baseball players, 15 basketball players, and 25 football players. In how many ways can you select one of each?

17. Suppose you are electing student council officers. The student council contains 24 students. In how many ways can a president, a vice-president, and a secretary be elected?

18. Suppose the code to a lock consists of three different numbers from the numbers 1 to 20, inclusive.

   a. How many three-number codes are possible?

   b. How many of the codes contain the numbers 6, 13, and 17?

19. A car dealer sells four different models of cars. Each of the cars can come in six different colors. For each of the cars, there are two different option packages available. In how many different ways can you select a car?

20. Teams in a math competition consist of six students. In how many ways can the six students be selected to work a problem on the board?

Practice 12-9

Simplify each expression.

1. $_9C_4$

2. $_{12}C_8$

3. $_9C_6$

4. $_{15}C_9$

5. $_{10}C_8$

6. $_{13}C_6$

7. $_{18}C_5$

8. $_{16}C_3$

9. $_{17}C_7$

10. $_9C_5$

11. $_{17}C_{13}$

12. $_{14}C_7$

13. A group of six tourists arrive at the airport 15 min before flight time. At the gate, they learn that only three seats are left on the airplane. How many different groups of three could get on the airplane?

14. In how many ways can you select 5 greeting cards from a choice of 12 cards at a store?

15. A committee of 4 students is to be formed from members of the student council. The student council contains 13 girls and 12 boys.

    a. How many different committees of four students are possible?

    b. How many committees will contain only boys?

    c. What is the probability that the committee will contain only boys?

16. Suppose your math class consists of 24 students. In how many ways can a group of 5 students be selected to form a math team?

17. A jar of marbles contains 6 yellow and 8 red marbles. Three marbles are selected at random.

    a. How many different groups of three marbles are possible?

    b. How many groups of three marbles will contain only red ones?

    c. What is the probability that the group of marbles will contain only red ones?

18. Suppose two members of your class need to be selected as members of the student council. Your class has 26 students in it. How many groups of two students can be selected?

19. The letters of the alphabet are written on slips of paper and placed in a hat. Three letters are selected at random.

    a. How many different combinations of three letters are possible?

    b. How many combinations consist only of the letters A, C, H, I, K, or Y?

    c. What is the probability that the letters selected consist only of the letters A, C, H, I, K, or Y?

20. Three boys and four girls are running for president and vice-president of the student council. What is the probability that a boy will be elected president and a girl will be elected vice-president?

21. A lottery requires that you match three numbers in order. The three numbers are chosen from the numbers 1–20. What is the probability that you will win this lottery if numbers can be chosen only once?